Elimination Communication Babies

PottyPlan

Elimination Communication Babies

PP
PottyPlan

Black + white ⊞ edition

From birth to toilet independence
A step-by-step plan

@eliminationcommunicationbabies

This revised edition published in 2021 by ChatterBox NZ Ltd.
First published in 2017 *Potty Plan*. Reprinted 202, 2021.

www.eliminationcommunicationbabies.com

This revised edition:

Softcover print on demand with black and white interior – UK English
ISBN 978-0-473-55443-9

Softcover print on demand with black and white interior – US English
ISBN 978-0-473-55518-4

Softcover print on demand with colour interior – UK English
ISBN 978-0-473-58616-4

Softcover print on demand with color interior – US English
ISBN 978-0-473-59693-4

Copyright © 2021 ChatterBox NZ Ltd.
Book design: www.chatterbox.net.nz

Dedication

This book is dedicated to your baby!

_____

We are committed to helping dedicated parents:

1. Build a strong bond through communication right from birth

2. Reduce nappy waste in our environment

3. Teach their children healthy, natural toileting practices

4. Save money.

**Head into this journey with a positive attitude.
Remember, everyone is different. Find your routine
and your baby's rhythm and have fun!**

Contents

Welcome

Acknowledgments

Hey there, I'm Rebecca – great to book-meet you!

Our family are from New Zealand and Canada. I stumbled upon the concept of Elimination Communication (EC) when living in Canada while I was pregnant. My partner and I thought it sounded awesome and that we should at least give it a try. When our baby responded immediately, we were *sold* on the concept! We were super low-key about it. We dressed our babies normally, used a flat-bottom bucket and did not obsess. We simply made going potty part of their normal daily routine right from birth.

Since we had so much fun with EC, and it helped our boys to reach toilet independence so young, we decided to share what we learned in a book that's simple to follow.

It can be overwhelming as a first-time parent. The way we live in Western culture, often separated from our family groups, means many of us don't have much to do with babies until we have one. Sometimes, being maternal does not come naturally, and many of us rely on marketing for advice. New parents need nurturing just as much as their new baby; however, we are barely in hospital long enough for a sandwich these days before being sent home to get on with it. I was fortunate to stay three nights when we had our first baby due to our footling breech C-section birth. Every time the baby needed feeding, I was able to call for assistance with latching. That support significantly helped with my confidence, and I only wish we could all get more support.

I hope that my work helps you in some way as a new parent.

As an Elimination Communication coach for hundreds of parents, I have been able to capture a wide range of experiences to enrich this book. I've built up a team of coaches who are just as passionate about sharing this technique. The book has been peer-reviewed, offering a collective range of tips and experiences. I've tried to keep this read as simple as possible for our tired and time-poor parents.

I want to send massive gratitude to everyone who has helped contribute to this passion project. To my husband, Mike, for his enthusiasm and encouragement of this project – you're an awesome EC dad! To my mum, Lorraine, for her endless support.

A big shout-out to our first daycare provider, Katy, at Happy Pals and the staff at Child's Wonder for being super supportive of EC for our children.

To Lauren Miller and Angela Hayes for the stunning photography sessions and modelling. A big thanks to the Bradshaws for the use of their very cool Kombi van. Thanks to Pāpāmoa Beach Resort for allowing us to shoot on site. This is a very meaningful location for our family.

I'm forever grateful for the motivation, help, ideas and input from my team of coaches and EC parents – Sonia Barrish, Alice Bockett, Bonnie Dening, Sara Dwyer, Jennifer Nickel, Melody Stewart, Heather Jenke, Chris, Mike and Melissa Gunn.

And, thank *you* for picking this book to start your EC journey with. I'm here for you, cheering you on!

Rebecca Larsen
Tauranga, New Zealand
September 2021

Foreword
by Clare Stead

"Give me a child until he is 7 and I will show you the man." — Aristotle, *The Philosophy of Aristotle*

Well, it turns out that although Aristotle was absolutely right that the man is made in childhood, he might well have been wrong about how long he needed the child for!

Rather than 7 years, he might just have needed that child for 1000 days to set them up for a lifetime of success! Isn't that amazing?!

Science is showing us that the first 1000 days of life, the time from conception to two is the most important for a child's development. It is a time when the brain is literally building itself and laying the foundations for all future learning for life. It's also the time that you, the baby's parents change from being a couple to becoming parents. There is a lot going on in that first 1000 days which is only 33 months!

What happens in the first 1000 days, what's affected and how do we know?

A baby's brain is doing amazing things really early on in pregnancy and it continues to develop throughout.

In a piece of brain tissue the size of a grain of rice, there are 10,000 nerve cells. Each one of those forms between 1 and 10,000 connections with other nerve cells.

There are an estimated one hundred trillion connections in a human brain.

At only four weeks gestation, a baby is creating neurons. These neurons are ones that will be used for their whole lives, from the very beginning through to the end of life. **By the time a woman is four weeks pregnant, 500,000 neurons are developing every minute.** These neurons build the brain layer by layer like an onion. They travel along supporting cells called glia in waves of millions of neurons. No other cells migrate in this way. There is some evidence that neurons have some idea where they need to travel to in the brain and that they also know whereabouts in the brain they are!

By the time a child is born their brain is about a quarter of the size of an average adult brain. Amazingly, it doubles in size in the first year of life and it keeps growing to about 80% of adult size by the age of 3 and by the time a child is 5 their brain is almost fully grown.

Their brain is formed in the womb, but the neural connections within that brain have yet to be connected. This happens through *the experiences* we give the child, even from before birth. At times during the first 1000 days of life, a child is developing 1 million synapse connections a second!

We know that the experiences and foundations that are laid down for a child in these first 1000 days affects their academic outcomes, their relationships, how much they will earn, what jobs they will do, how the adult they will become thinks and even their health.

So, the experiences that we give babies from conception onwards really do matter.

This book is all about Elimination Communication. Rebecca talks about communication both verbal and nonverbal, routine, play, success and independence. All of these skills are vital when teaching your child elimination communication, but they are also the foundation skills for many other areas in life.

All learning is done from the simple to the complex; we build a foundation of learning that we can build other skills on top of. Our babies need to learn everything, and they do this through play and the experiences that we give them. When we understand the impact that tiny activities we do have on our baby's brain development, we naturally want to do more of it. Because we do more, we build our baby's brain connections and help them become stronger which in turn helps our child reach their full potential. It's really clever, it's simple, but the impact it has on your child is massive.

Our children learn best in an environment of loving relationships. When we have secure relationships, our child feels secure and able to learn, grow and develop. Helping your child reach their full potential is about providing them with stimulating tiny activities every day that help them build one tiny skill on a previous skill. The activities you do with your baby may look simple to you, but to your baby they really are brain building.

Your journey in elimination communication is providing your baby with tiny experiences that will support their learning and brain building in so many other ways (such as their language development, their physical development, their independence, their problem solving and quite possibly even their mathematical understanding). As you take the time to watch your child, talk with them, hold them out etc, you are also building a really strong bond, you are learning more about your child and that will help them feel secure, loved and enable them to begin to develop in so many other ways. It will also help you understand them better, react to their needs better and respond appropriately.

It's only 1000 days but they are 1000 days that last a lifetime!

About Clare Stead

Clare Stead, Founder and Director of **Oliiki Ltd** and mother of three, is an e-learning specialist, education researcher and qualified primary school teacher. Clare built the Oliiki app to support parents through the most important days of a child's development to help their child reach their full potential. The Oliiki app can be found in both the Apple and the Android app stores.

Her website is **www.oliiki.com**.

'Cause babies *can* potty!

Section 1 – 'Cause babies *can* potty!

This journey is a natural assisted progression toward toilet independence. You won't be dealing with sh!t for an unmerciful amount of time or spending a crapload on nappy wearing and setting your baby up for unhealthy toileting habits or related distressing conditions. Section 1 is an overview of Elimination Communication. If you want to jump straight into the how-to, flick through to section 3.

What is Elimination Communication?

Elimination is poo and pee or whatever you call it, **Communication** is a two-way conversation. Elimination Communication is a gentle assisted method for offering baby toilet opportunities, progressing toward toilet independence through a healthy and respectful approach. This is not a new concept, and it is widely practised worldwide; however, the term Elimination Communication is relatively new. In her book *Diaper Free: The Gentle Wisdom of Natural Infant Hygiene* (2001), author Ingrid Bauer penned the term Elimination Communication.

With *Elimination Communication Babies* you will be introducing toilet practice to your baby using natural timing and communication. Following natural elimination rhythms and instinct, it is easy to assist your baby. Your baby will learn this quickly. You will use cues and communication to encourage your baby. We recommend that you still use nappies but consider them as 'back-up'. You can ditch the nappies with more observation and assistance if you're fully immersed!

Stage one – The EC hold

The baby cannot sit, is on a liquid diet and is assisted in eliminating in a held squat position over a potty. The old term for this is 'held out'. The baby does instinctively eliminate when in this hold and can show signals when they need to eliminate. The EC hold is a deep squat and a very advantageous position for passing stool. This stage is important as it reduces the risk of nappy rash/nappy dermatitis, soft tissue infections or worse, MRSA.[1] It builds communication between baby and parent. Natural elimination patterns are responded to, resulting in a cleaner and healthier practice.

Regular potty use maintains and develops sphincter control from a young age.[2] The baby also follows their instinctual preference to eliminate outside their clothing or bedding and learns correct potty use. Nappies are worn as a back-up and not solely worn for the duty of being a toilet. The use of a nappy forms a habit that must otherwise be unlearned.

Stage two – The sitting potty

The baby can sit unsupported and is eating solid foods. Once a baby can sit without being supported, they can control and coordinate their bladder, urethral sphincter and anal sphincter muscles.[3] The potty is used as an accessible, safe option during this stage and encourages a squat sitting position. This stage is important for healthy stool elimination and early development in toilet independence. A baby can begin to get onto and off of the potty independently. Regular use of the potty develops the elimination routine and can be beneficial to avoid urinary tract infections.[4,5]

Stage three – Toilet independence (toilet training)

The toddler can walk and communicate. This final stage progresses the child through using the toilet assisted to non-assisted where the child can state their need to go toilet before they go. For Elimination Communication children, this final stage focuses on bladder control and recognising their need to use the toilet. The bladder can now hold more, and the frequency of urination is less. For children starting their toilet learning here, the process of stool management sometimes follows bladder control. Privacy and independence become important for a child as they become more self-aware. This stage is important as it is the final stage to toilet independence and removal of the nappy safety net. On average (EC children) reach daytime dryness around 18 months and bowel control from 6 months.[6,7]

Stage four – Sleep dryness

Nighttime assistance can occur during the first three stages or following. Nighttime dryness can be achieved earlier if started earlier. It's fair enough to prioritise sleep though. You may wait until your child can walk and aid themself to the toilet. While encouraging independence, you will still need to offer assistance and provide lighting and tools for their success. Aim to wrap up nighttime before too long, so night wetting does not become a habit. Deep sleepers may need nighttime assistance. EC children are thought to have better awareness and control of the bladder, with more complete emptying. Anecdotally, they have less nocturnal enuresis (bed-wetting).[8]

C-R-C -- our winning EC formula

Communication, **R**outine, **C**onsistency.

Communication

Communication is a two-way conversation, and it is also about listening. The first 1000 days, from conception to the second birthday, are a time of massive development and of vital importance. Nourish your baby's mental, emotional and physical health during this time for lifelong health and well-being. Elimination Communication falls right within this timeframe and is a perfect reason to engage with toilet assistance during this beneficial time.

When the baby is being held out in the early stages, a cue you might use could be a sound like 'psst' or a whistle, or you can simply use a word. We've seen fun adaptions made by parents with their cues to baby, which make us and baby giggle, for example, using a 'fart app' to cue. EC is fun!

Your communication and assistance are essential. Talk to your baby about what you are doing and why. Use the proper terms for their elimination, if you prefer. Your voice will soothe them, and they will develop an understanding. Also, give your baby a chance to process. Some quiet pauses as you talk can help.

Communication is also conveyed through your body language, your facial expressions and your general mood. This is important to remember, especially if you are tired or stressed. So try to be relaxed and confident.

Your baby will also communicate with you. This will start with natural signals such as body language and vocal noises. Before your baby can talk, you can introduce non-verbal language such as baby sign language. Waving goodbye is one example of this. There are fantastic resources online for baby sign language. Some common signs to learn are 'potty', 'all done', 'more', 'drink', 'eat', 'book'.

Before your baby can talk, they will understand you. When they're nearing the toddler stage, you'll use simple instruction. All the time, they are moving toward toilet independence, where they will eventually communicate their toilet needs verbally with you. The communication evolves like this:

• Parent uses a sound or word cue at potty time. The parent watches for the baby's natural elimination signals. Every child will signal before they eliminate, but it might be as subtle as a snail winking.

• Baby begins to use non-verbal communication to indicate elimination, but not always – this needs to be taught, and they may just not do it. The parent communicates verbally about what and why.

- Child begins simple verbal communication and can eventually string together a sentence. Non-verbal and verbal can happen simultaneously. The parent offers simple, encouraging direction allowing time for reflection.

- Eventually, your child will just head off to the toilet until you get the bum wipe call.

Routine

Routine helps babies understand their world, and fitting Elimination Communication into their daily routine helps make it a normal part of their lives.

Consistency

If you can offer consistency, your baby will rely on these opportunities to eliminate. Remember, a break can create a new habit, and a habit can take time to break, but don't freak out if you have some breaks. It's all good practise.

Praise or reward

To guide your child effectively, they need to understand what's right or wrong so they get it right. Wrong does not mean bad. This can be understood through your tone and

Be like a postage stamp. Stick to a thing till you get there.

facial expressions. Generally, praise is very effective at getting this message across. It does not have to be a big song and dance. Whatever comes naturally for you will be fine. Some parents don't agree with praise but should still communicate what is expected in some way. However you choose to do it, be consistent.

Reward yourself? – why not – as you won't need to bribe or reward your baby. Once it's time to buy toddler underwear, that could be perceived as rewarding for your toddler.

Who can assist with elimination?

Elimination Communication can be offered by either parent or trusted caregiver until a child reaches a stage where privacy is requested.

If you are a working parent, your caregiver ideally should assist with Elimination Communication following our basic routine approach. Before enrolling with a caregiver, interview them to see if they would be willing to continue this care. Establishing your routines with Elimination Communication can be advantageous for at least your baby's first year.

If you are sharing care duties, it is best to be consistent with the approach you take. Most centres will be happy to provide families with specific care requirements and should accommodate Elimination Communication. We will share an easy routine, that will help with consistency.

Remember, assisting your baby with anything is about you

and your level of commitment or ability to do it. Much like feeding, a baby needs help. Every baby can do this. It takes a parent to assist and guide them. Your child will be more successful with your *committed* guidance and assistance. You've got this, and your baby is lucky to have you!

Timing and baby's signals

> The most common age for a baby to *intentionally* communicate elimination needs is 12 months.[9]

Offer the potty consistently and routinely based on natural elimination timings, and also watch for elimination signals from your baby. You can then add in more transitional timing opportunities if required. We'd like to stress that you shouldn't overdo it or worry about missing pee catches until you focus on that in stage three. Urine frequently happens until the bladder is larger. The importance is the communication, the practice and toilet association, and a bonus is that poo is an easy 'catch'.

Observation time is a period where a baby is observed (usually without the nappy on) to watch for their *natural* **elimination signals**. Once you learn your baby's natural signals, you can then watch out for them. Signals can be 'pulling off' when feeding (distraction), glassy eyes, shivering, gas, grizzles or grunts. You may also feel your baby tense up slightly. When the baby is in a carrier or sling, they may push away from the parent. Some people notice that their baby also fusses when needing a change or becomes upset before eliminating. *Don't get stuck observing* if you don't see anything. We recommend that you start EC based on a timing routine to get established. Some babies are incredibly subtle with their signals. As you progress, you can teach them some non-verbal signals. They may then use these signals intentionally.

Natural timing is generally after feeding, sometimes during feeding when babies are very young. A hand held style potty can be offered while feeding.

Transitional timing refers to a change of scene before a bath, a car ride, going to sleep or waking up.

Part-time or full-time

Part-time EC can be interpreted as offering assistance for part of the time. For example, only at home or on weekends.

Elimination Communication Babies outlines a full-time approach but acknowledges that any assistance is positive. It is fantastic that Elimination Communication can be offered part-time or full-time. Our recommendation is to offer consistently, if you can, to avoid mixed messages.

Whatever your approach, be consistent and reliable with it. This does not mean you will catch every pee or poo. It is your commitment to offering assistance consistently and the communication that will help your baby the most.

If you cannot offer full-time EC during the day, consider getting assistance provided by your caregiver. Otherwise, do your best to introduce the concept as much as you can.

Siblings

A baby and a toddler can be pottied together routinely. It's very manageable if your toddler is happy to sit with you while you hold out your baby. Keep your toddler engaged in conversation, and provide things to hold on to. Involve them in the process with the baby, explaining what you are doing and why. Ask them for help, like passing you a cloth.

Suppose you are starting Elimination Communication with your second or later baby and currently have a toddler who is not potty trained. In that case, it can help the toddler to watch and learn as the baby is assisted. Your toddler can have their own potty, which can be set up beside you as you EC your baby. With encouragement, your toddler may take an interest. Start offering the potty to your toddler routinely, just as you will be doing with your newborn.

Eventually, a younger child will often show more confidence in using the potty or toilet as they have had the opportunity to watch their older sibling. Naturally, they may want to try and achieve the same as their older sibling, so Elimination Communication can get easier. This phenomenon can also happen in care centres where toddlers will want to copy their peers. Our 12-month-old used his potty in our small daycare, and it did not take long before his peers wanted to try too. Use this to your advantage! On average, younger siblings complete training sooner.[10]

Multiples

Give it a try as best you can, but don't stress, this is a journey. During stage one, the hold out stage, if you are feeding simultaneously, offer to one baby then the other after feeding. Keep your change mat and potty handy. You can place one baby to kick on the change mat while offering the potty to the other. Give them both a chance to dry before putting the nappy back on.

If you decide to offer the potty upon waking up, you may be able to offer it to one baby while the other is sleeping.

The easiest scenario for twins will be a portable top hat style potty or a flat bucket that you can use where you are assisting with feeding to watch over both babies while attending to one.

Find your own rhythm. Any Elimination Communication you can offer is positive.

Once they can sit, you may find it easier to potty them together. If they are very active, keep them busy with toys and engage with them while pottying. Take turns if you need to. If it's too much to manage, step it back a notch. You're incredible!

Time	15 cents/unit	30 cents/unit	45 cents/unit
6 months = 1440 nappies	$216	$432	$648
12 months = 2880 nappies	$432	$864	$1296
18 months = 4320 nappies	$648	$1296	$1944
24 months = 5760 nappies	$864	$1728	$2592
2.5 years = 7200 nappies	$1080	$2160	$3241
3 years = 8640 nappies	$1296	$2592	$3888
3.5 years = 10,080 nappies	$1512	$3024	$4536

Assuming 8 changes daily

This table illustrates the potential expense and volume if using disposable nappies. Over the years, our Western society has moved steadily into consumer culture, leaving behind skills and knowledge. Consequently, our cost of living is higher. It is simply not true that disposables are more convenient when it prolongs the time spent wearing them. Disposables are practical for incontinence or other medical issues, however. Healthy children can be assisted and successful at using toilets much sooner than society and industry have us believe. Disposables are big business, a $71 billion a year industry. An estimated *20 billion diapers (nappies) enter landfills each year*, making up over 4% of solid landfill waste and are the third-largest single consumer item in landfills.[11]

Challenge: If you are using cloth, keep track of the number of changes on a whiteboard. Each is a disposable you have saved from a landfill. Sharing inspires others!
Tag us at @eliminationcommunicationbabies.

The decline of the potty – a timeline

1596   The flush toilet was invented, but not widely used yet.[12]

1851   The flush toilet became more widespread. Before this time, the majority of people used chamber pots (a potty), holes in the ground or communal outhouses.[13]

Cultures worldwide would 'hold a baby out' over a bowl or the ground to urinate or defecate until they could sit on a potty or squat. This potty method was common in Western culture until a shift occurred after the world wars.

1914-18 World War I.

1920s   Rigid and strict toilet training methods were promoted in some countries during the 1920s and 1930s.[14]

1930s   Sigmund Freud, Austrian neurologist and the founder of psychoanalysis, introduced the idea that babyhood 'trauma' gives rise to mental illness in adulthood.[15]

1939-45 World War II.

1940s   Anthropologist and author Geoffrey Gorer, hired by the U.S. Office of War to analyse the 'enemy,' reasoned that Japanese parents potty train their babies earlier than Western parents and that this accounted for "the overwhelming brutality and sadism of the Japanese at war."[16]

After WWII, more women entered the workforce. There is a marketing push on formula, commercial baby food and nappies, now mass-produced.

1946   American paediatrician Dr Benjamin Spock published an influential book, *The Common Sense Book of Baby and Child Care*, which urged parents to leave bowel training almost entirely up to their baby.[17]

1946–64 Baby boom period.

1947   UK's first disposable nappy, the Paddi, was invented by Valerie Gordon-Hunter.

1950   Until the mid-1900s the majority of (Western) babies finished toilet training by two years and achieved nighttime dryness by three years.

1950s   Gerber (and others) targeted baby food advertising to the medical community who were influential in helping promote feeding solids to newborns.[18]

1955   Disposable diaper (nappy) first patented in the US.[19]

1956   La Leche League formed.

1962   Paediatric developmental specialist Dr T. Berry Brazelton published a seminal paper outlining why parents should avoid pushing their child prematurely to toilet training.[20] Dr Brazelton was also a spokesperson and consultant for American nappy company Pampers, advising on the larger-sized nappies and appearing in advertising for size 6 nappies.

1970   The rise of the disposable nappy industry.[21]

1980   By the 1980s most US families use disposable nappies. Family lives are busier and disposables are considered convenient.[22]

2000   By the early 2000s the average age that (Western) parents recognised their child showed an interest in using the potty was 24–25 months. Daytime dryness was achieved on average at almost 3 years of age. Nighttime accidents are considered normal until 5 or 6 years of age.

2001   Ingrid Bauer penned the term Elimination Communication in her book Diaper Free: The Gentle Wisdom of Natural Infant Hygiene (2001).

2007   Pampers, a disposable nappy company, releases a nappy for children who weigh more than 18 kilograms (the average weight of a 5-year-old).[23]

Now   The effects of global warming are being felt around the globe. Consumerism is embraced; however, there is a shift toward sustainable living. Are parents ready for EC?

It's important to recognise that the coercive approach that doctors rejected in the early 1900s has resulted in a movement away from any guided assistance for babies. Consequently, the marketing push to delay toilet training fell into place with the backing of doctors – a trusted source.

We need to recognise that it was not the early practice but the forceful approach that needed to change. Delayed toilet training can increase the risk of bladder problems[24] and stool toileting refusal, which can lead to stool withholding and primary encopresis.[25]

Punishment and trauma are still apparent for some children despite delayed toilet training. The fundamentals of Elimination Communication are instinctual, gentle and respectful.

Delayed toilet training and, consequently, more frequent toilet training issues are possibly because of our much busier lifestyles and relaxed attitudes. Saying "I'll start when my child is ready" can dismiss adult accountability. The result of constant messaging that supports waiting is trusted and not questioned. Parents a generation or two back generally had one parent in the role of home-maker, and the pace was less hectic. Disposable nappies were more expensive, and parents used a potty. Many parents nowadays start their children on the toilet, skipping two stages and the potty.

A relaxed attitude can mean some parents start potty training when their child is more self-aware, which can be challenging for some children. Elimination Communication is advantageous as babies are easier to potty, and it's generally wrapped up before the time when self-awareness can cause resistance.

What's in it for me to EC? We asked...

Benefits for the EC parent

- Faster bum changes

- Less chance of a poonami

- Less unexpected pooping

- Less nappy rash to deal with

- No scrubbing poopy cloth

- I'm making greener choices for our family

- I'm saving money buying fewer nappies

- Happier baby – he hates soiling himself

- Building an association with the potty so it's not so scary later on

- Respecting my baby and his communication, just like letting me know when he's hungry or tired

And this:

- You don't have to scrub doo off your littlie's folds/rolls/ cracks and crevasses. Just a simple wipe of the hiney.

The average burden versus satisfaction of elimination communication, on a scale of 1 (Not satisfied) to 10 (Totally satisfied) is 8.5 with most participants claiming total satisfaction.[26]

#EliminationCommunicationBabies

What's in it
for baby to EC?
We asked...

Benefits for the EC baby

- I'll have less chance of nappy rash

- I'm less likely to poop in my nappies most of the time

- I'll be easy to take out, as my parents will know when I'll most likely need to poop

- I'm less likely to fear the big toilet when I become a toddler

- I'm less likely to withhold stool and develop constipation issues because I'm comfortable using a toilet

- I'll most likely be out of nappies between ages 1 and 2

- I'll be able to completely empty my bladder and bowel easier and have less chance of urinary tract infections

- With regular elimination assistance, I'll be developing sphincter control without being delayed

- I'll be a happier and healthier baby and learn ways to communicate my needs, and feel confident my needs are being listened to

The main motivation to practise EC was feeling it was more respectful for the baby.[27]

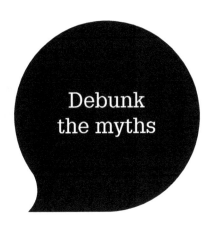

Debunk
the myths

Babies should not be encouraged to hold on

Elimination Communication never encourages holding on. In fact, the opposite – the baby is offered the chance to completely empty regularly. Excessive holding on is an issue that can cause encopresis (serious constipation) and can happen to *any* child when there is anxiety with pooping. Some learners will hold on to stool due to 'fear' of the toilet or may experience a painful poo, then become anxious. Because Elimination Communication is a gentle guided progression, we are less likely to see issues with holding on. Babies and toddlers who are given the opportunity to eliminate regularly on toilets or a potty will develop healthy toileting skills. We need to watch our Western diets and keep our little ones regular.

> In a study comparing healthy Vietnamese (where toilet training is started in infancy and nappies are infrequently used) and Swedish children,[28] the authors observed that early potty training of Vietnamese children led to complete bladder emptying by 9 months of age, while Swedish children did not show complete emptying until the age of 36 months (when they were toilet trained). By the age of

24 months, 98% of Vietnamese children had achieved
bladder control independent of support from an adult,
while by the age of 36 months, only 55% of Swedish
children had reached this milestone.[29]

Children should potty train when they are ready

This message is ingrained in our culture, but a baby is
ready from the get-go! Baby poo is very liquid and backed
with gas so that it projects away from their skin. It's fantastic
that we're built for EC! Waiting for the child to mature
instead teaches them to use clothing as a toilet. Young
babies may eliminate on a change mat or grizzle before
they need to eliminate – all signs they are trying to give us
to ask for assistance. The next step is sitting to eliminate
when their poo is more solid. When sitting on the potty, a
baby does control the release of their poo and pee. It does
not just fall out randomly.

A complete bladder and bowel emptying can reduce the
risk of urinary tract infection.[30] Regular potty use maintains
and develops sphincter control from a young age. The
dyscoordination between the sphincter and detrusor muscle
seems to have already disappeared at the age of 9 months
in infants who are potty trained very early.[31]

Elimination Communication and potty training are also
different. The word, training, describes the approach taken
when the child needs to re-learn where to eliminate after
their whole life using a nappy. Elimination Communication
children are also potty trained during the toddler stage
once the child is walking and when their bladder can hold

more and they can stay dry longer. We call this stage 'toilet independence', some prefer 'toilet learning'.

It's too much work, and it's messy

For the most part, babies and toddlers are a lot of work. They require a lot of assistance and care. Elimination Communication can fit into your daily routines. Because the baby is using a potty, poop is easier to clean up. It can be argued that cleaning a soiled nappy and scrubbing clothing clean is also very time-consuming. One complaint often seen online is about nappies leaking. Consider the additional bedding and clothing changes that can be mostly avoided through the use of Elimination Communication. The choice is for the parent to make, and whichever they choose should be respected.

> 1155 participants rated how tiring and/or time-consuming they felt EC was on a scale of 1 (not tiring or time-consuming at all) to 10 (enormously tiring or time-consuming). Most people rated 3, with a mean of 3.9.[32]

18 months of potty training versus 2 weeks when the child is actually ready

Elimination Communication is not potty training, and many children are not potty trained by 18 months. Many are still using nappies at age 3 or older, which requires nappy changes over the years. There is a misconception that Elimination Communication is time-consuming. EC babies are generally toilet independent sooner, meaning fewer nappies and fewer changes overall.

Let the baby be a baby

Babies naturally hold their elimination for a short while like all mammals, and they naturally don't want to eliminate on themselves. Elimination Communication is about providing a baby with the opportunity to eliminate somewhere other than in their clothing. It's a respectful choice.

EC adds more stress

Stress can be affected by external factors. Many parents report positive experiences with Elimination Communication. If it were to become an external factor that caused you stress, you could quickly stop. Your mental health matters first!

> Participants were asked if they had completely stopped practicing EC during a certain period of time (at least a week) and then resumed EC. Most participants said no (71.4%).
>
> Only 2.4% claimed they had definitively abandoned EC. Their reasons were predominantly due to lack of success and potty refusal, but participants also mentioned stress and domestic or external workload, lack of support, depression, or anxiety.
>
> Approximately half of the 1160 participants practised daytime EC part-time and half fulltime.[33]

Meet the mess.

Meet Pee!

Urine, Pee, Wee-Wee, Widdles, Piddles, Number One

Pee is nice if you treat her right but don't push her limits.

Her goal is to stay liquid – she aims to land in the potty or toilet if she can. Watch out if she gets soaked up. That's when she can turn nasty. She'll make delicate skin burn if left too long and cause a real stink. She's OK; just treat her right, and she won't bother you too much. She loves to be flushed – 'weeeeeeeeee' she will say, so sometimes she's also called 'Wee'. Don't worry about Pee; she has a mind of her own. One day when the time is right, and you remove her safety net, she will make her waterfall splash that she's always dreamed about.

Newborns pee frequently. Over time pee consolidates. After a toddler is walking, there is further growth of the bladder. At this point, alongside some wetness toilet training, a child can manage their pee and control their bladder.

Meet Seedy!

Speedy Seedy is very sweet and loves to make us smile.

This busy character is always working on something big and rushing from one thing to another. Seedy is a regular friend, usually visiting right after a meal and sometimes in the middle of it. He can be a real messy character at times, especially if you're are not quite ready for his visit.

Seedy's favourite game is 'hit the target'. If he does not get to play target practice, he'll get rather explosive.
Watch out, or he will **'*!BOOM!*'** and with his artistic talent, he'll paint everything sweet sticky yellow.

Meet Whiffy!

Flatulence, Fart, Toot, Pop, Fluffy, Honker, Ripper

You're going to love Whiffy, your Elimination Communication best friend. Whiffy has a funny way of getting attention by getting right up your nose! Sometimes loud, sometimes silent, always potent and always brings a smile!

Whiffy loves to hang around. Sometimes with the dog, sometimes with you, sometimes with your baby and even with the Queen. Whiffy knows he's the only one allowed in your underwear!

We love Whiffy too! Whiffy is always out front, shape-shifting and sneaking to the front of his BFF Poo. When Whiffy turns up, Poo is not far behind. Whiffy has many friends, all with unique traits: Pop, Fluff, Windy, Toot and Gassy and a few.

Fine-tune your sense of smell and be on high alert for Whiffy when you are doing Elimination Communication. Whiffy will help you prepare in advance to catch Poo safely and avoid Squish.

Meet Poo!

Faeces, Stool, Plops, Poops, Doo-Doo, Number Two

For the most part, Poo is a fairly solid character.

His goal is to please. He much prefers to make an appearance in a potty or with a splash. If this is not an option, he becomes 'Squish' who you will meet later, and Squish is a bit of a stink.

Poo can be a routine chap, generally visiting at least once a day and often after food is served. But not always – sometimes he's a little unreliable. But don't worry – he will show up, and his friends Pop, Fluff and Whiffy usually sneak out first, giving you a chance to get ready for his arrival.

One of the great things about Elimination Communication is that Poo is easy to manage. Children who are assisted with Elimination Communication will learn stool control first. Children should be regular and ideally passing at least one poo daily once they are eating solids.

Meet Squish!

#SolidMess

Poosplosion, Poonami, Shitastrophe, Shantz, Pooted

You're probably going to meet Squish at some point on your
Elimination Communication journey, but hopefully,
he won't turn up too often.

He ruins clothes, he leaves a mark to show he's been, and he's
a right stinker. It's incredible how far he can spread up the back
and down the legs. He's just trying to get out and find his toilet,
but it's challenging for him when things get in his way. All he
wants to do is swim the sewer pipes to the land of his dreams.
When he's balled up and tossed out, he'll do all he can to be
rescued by releasing his potent fumes.

Elimination Communication helps you avoid meeting up with
Squish too much – phew!

💩 Before baby arrives

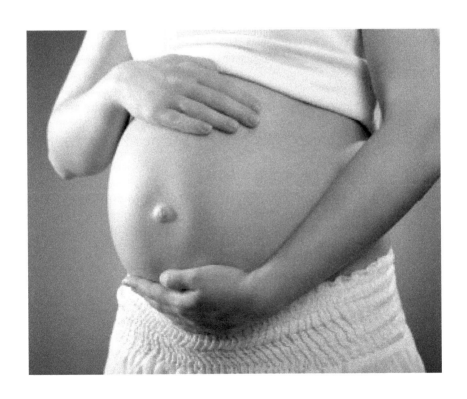

Section 3 – Before baby arrives

Congratulations! Your baby will be here with you very soon, learning all about eating, playing, sleeping, bonding with family, and, of course, eliminating. What a journey!

Elimination Communication Babies focuses on establishing a routine around natural elimination patterns and watching for elimination signals from your baby. You will allow your baby ample opportunities to eliminate. This method is natural, safe and easy to learn.

Elimination Communication is fun! You will celebrate every new thing your baby does, from the first smiles to the first steps. When they start using the potty, you will be just as excited – we encourage you to share this method!

Don't buy:

- An expensive nappy bucket with refill bags/cassettes.

- Nappy-rash cream. Wait to see if you need it first.

- Talc powder – air-drying is best.

The potty set-up

Baby is almost here, and I bet you can't wait! Even if you're planning a home birth, keep a bag packed just in case with your supplies, some newborn-sized nappies, wipes and some huge comfy black undies for

Consistency is key!
EC is:
Healthier
Easier
Faster
Cheaper
Rewarding.

Hatty
#MyFirstPotty

yourself. A little olive oil is a healthy substitute for Vaseline around a baby's delicate skin, where wetness can cause rash or skin irritation. Baby will need changing approximately every two hours as a newborn, so you will become a change expert in no time.

Your potty set-up will consist of an area to potty baby, including a potty/bucket, an area where baby can air-dry and a place to put the nappy back on. In some houses, more than one potty and change area will be helpful.

What you will need:

- Decide on a toilet/potty/bowl for baby, or use several.
- Spray cleaner and a cleaning brush. Sodium percarbonate for a natural steriliser.
- Wipe cloths.
- A change table or waterproof change pad for the floor.
- A portable change pad for your nappy bag.
- Towels or cotton blankets for your baby to lie on.
- Your choice of nappies as back-up.
- A wet bag for cloth nappies.
- A liner to protect bedding.

○   Olive oil is a perfect lubricant for delicate skin.

○   EC-easy clothing.

You don't need a lot of 'stuff' to offer the potty. Select equipment that is simple and easy to clean. Keep it simple.

Any container that can fit in a sink, or on the floor such as a flat-bottom bucket.

A top hat potty can be useful at the newborn stage. A potty cosy can be added to the rim.

A simple one-piece potty is perfect once baby is sitting

A simple easy-to-clean seat reducer may be needed from when baby can stand.

A change mat you place on the floor for bare bottom time.

An easy-clean foam floor mat protects your knees and flooring from spills.

! IMPORTANT !
Consistent action
creates
consistent results
! IMPORTANT !

Change table set-up

Having a changing table set up is an organised way to have everything handy for change time; however, you will frequently be moving from the toilet or potty to the change table. It is more convenient to use the change mat on the ground near the potty and sink location. While at home, try using running water or wet cloths as a substitute for disposable wipes. Baby wipes can be an irritant on some sensitive skin and lead to additional waste and expense. You should not need to use any barrier creams where no rash is present, and if you do need to use a mild moisturiser around the sensitive groin area, a good natural alternative is olive or coconut oil (test on a patch of skin first).

The importance of bare-bum floor time

Wet and soiled nappies against the skin can cause nappy rash, and the best way to prevent it is to get babies out of nappies. Creams and wipes can further irritate nappy dermatitis.[12] Bare-bum time allows your baby to dry out naturally, keeping everything down there nice and healthy. If you do happen to experience rash symptoms but are offering ample dry-out time, acidic food reactions (in later months) or a yeast

'Peach Time'

infection (thrush) could be a cause, in which case you would need to seek medical support. Keep up the bare-bum routine to dry out your baby before putting a nappy back on, especially newborns. Put bare-bum baby on their tummy for 'peach time', which helps to strengthen the back and tummy muscles. Always be watchful for any struggles on the tummy. This free bare-bum time on the change mat, placed on the floor, is the perfect time for your baby to kick, wriggle, and eventually learn to roll over.

Avoid rash: **After a toilet offer, always allow your baby to dry off before putting the nappy on.** So important!

Cloth and EC together

Cloth and Elimination Communication together are the most sustainable and economic approaches. You can also manage the poo easily with Elimination Communication, dealing with primarily wet nappies to wash.

Some people will choose to use disposables part-time, such as with a newborn (until poo is managed) or overnight only. By cutting down your consumption, you'll save money and reduce nappies going into landfills.

When selecting a nappy system, it is a personal choice, and they will need to fit your baby's body shape. For Elimination Communication, you will want to consider how easy they are to remove. Other considerations are how many parts there are to a system, how easy they are to wash and dry, and the absorbency.

Nappy belt: Worn around your baby's waist to hold folded flats or a prefold in place. Useful until baby is walking. Easy to remove for toilet time. Best used at home and once poo is managed to avoid a blow-out.

Flats: Flat squares of fabric (traditional nappy) folded and fastened onto baby. Cheapest option. Easy to wash. Requires folding, fasteners, a cover (not waterproof), or a nappy belt (around the home). Dries fast.

Prefolds: Flat squares of fabric with thicker middle panel sewn in. Easy to wash. Requires some easy folding, fasteners and a cover (not waterproof). Use with a nappy belt or fasteners.

Fitteds: Not waterproof nappy with sewn-in elastics. Closes with snaps or Velcro, requires covers. Very absorbent, slow to dry. Not an ideal system for EC, requiring two systems to remove for toileting. Useful for overnight wear if not offering the toilet during nighttime.

Covers: Water-resistant outer for non-waterproof nappies. Can be re-used if not wet. Natural wool options are available. Dome or Velcro options. Velcro is slightly easier to put on/take off but not as easy to adjust for sizing around the legs. Watch Velcro with other washing. Use with flats, prefolds and fitteds.

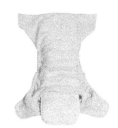

Pockets: Nappy with waterproof cover sewn in. A fabric pocket for stuffing inserts. Useful for overnight wear if not offering the toilet during nighttime. Often a change during the night if feeding is a good idea. Easy to remove.

All-in-two: Nappy with waterproof cover sewn in. Inserts lay-in or snap-in, which allows for easier washing, and natural or cotton inserts to feel wetness. More flexibility for EC and easy to remove.

All-in-one: The waterproof cover, inserts and fasteners are all sewn together. Slower drying. Convenient, easy to remove.

Drop-flap nappy: Nappies made for Elimination Communication. Used up until toddler is walking. Drop down the waterproof flap to offer the potty, or quickly change the absorbent pad inside. Quick to dry.

Drop-flap nappy: The duo belt and pocket-base system by Flappy Nappies makes a potty break quick and easy. Flaps open from the front or back. Quick to dry.

Training pants and underwear: Pull-up padded or thick fabric underwear perfect for walkers or very active toddlers who don't want to lie down for a nappy change. Wool soakers are an option to use over top of thick underwear. Wool repels water naturally.

Cloth swim nappy: For your baby swim lessons. Pocket nappies that have lost their waterproofing can work in place of a swim nappy.

Cloth set-up

Your cloth set-up will be unique for you. Here are some ideas for a collection with easy washing and minimal waste.

A cloth set-up which includes flats, covers, cloth wipes and some compostables.

Nine flats and cover combo nappy changes, and only one cover needed washing.

Minimal waste and a healthier practice. Pictures @clothcrew_chc

Quick to wash and easy to dry.

Which fabric?

Nappies come in a variety of fabric options. Here are some of the fabric options available.

Wool is an excellent natural water repellent, sustainable and biodegradable. Usually available as a cover or outer layer, belt, and also used to line cribs.

Cotton is absorbent and offers a wet feel. Cotton is sustainable, renewable and biodegradable, making it an excellent choice as an environmentally friendly fabric.

Bamboo fabric (rayon from bamboo) is a man-made fabric created from natural materials. It is soft and very absorbent. Not biodegradable.

Microfibres are a man-made synthetic (polyester and nylon) soft fabric designed to repel wetting and offer a dry feeling. It is quick-drying and easy to care for. Not biodegradable.

A disposable nappy washed up at a beach after a storm.

It's estimated that single-use nappies take 500 years to decompose in a landfill.[34]

Selecting for the stages

There are three nappy stages your baby will graduate through. The newborn stage is where wetting is smaller but frequent and poo is runny. The next stage will take you up to walking and is when most of your nappy-wearing occurs. Pull-ups/trainers are worn usually by the time your toddler is walking.

How much cloth?

This is a guide only. Some people will use disposables during the newborn stage or at nighttime and cloth during the day. How much cloth you use can vary based on your baby's pee volume and your laundry routine. Inserts will allow for further flexibility and can be counted as a change or rotation. This guide provides for laundry every other day.

Newborn stage:
10–15 changes daily, 21–24 in rotation
 e.g. 7 nappies/21 inserts or 21 nappies

Nappy stage (3 months to walking):
5–10 changes, 20 in rotation

Pull-up stage:
4–8 changes, 16 in rotation

Underwear:
10–14 in rotation

> If all you do is follow the herd, you'll just be stepping in poop all day.
> Wayne Dyer

Keeping it clean

Dry pailing and washing cloth – there's a hole in my bucket

Use a bucket or basket that has holes in it – such as a dedicated laundry basket. Closed buckets encourage ammonia build-up resulting in foul odours and possible damage to your cloth. Buckets that can breathe or aerate will create less smell.

Wet nappies can be placed directly into your dry pail. Optionally, rinse the nappies, especially if you are not washing frequently. If the nappy is soiled, scrape waste into the toilet – this goes for disposables as well. For both soiled or overnight cloth nappies, a thorough hand rinse is recommended before dry pailing. A bidet/nappy sprayer attached to the toilet is convenient for rinsing cloth nappies.

A natural way to sterilise the potty and nappies

Sodium percarbonate is a safe, natural steriliser you can purchase from a bulk bin or home brewing store. You can add a tablespoon into a potty with water to sterilise or add in 1–4 tablespoons to a load of nappies with your washing detergent and select the soak cycle on your machine. Soaking nappies every so often overnight in sodium percarbonate can remove some staining. Air-dry in the sun stain side out to remove any further staining if this is possible in your climate.

Keeping a dedicated potty cleaning brush and your choice of spray cleaner is also a quick and easy option for cleaning the potty.

Nappy-free

Our approach relies on nappy back-up while offering the toilet until the child is independent with the hope to share a straightforward process with more people. If you're planning to try a nappy-free approach, these principles still apply, but you may need to offer more frequently. You will also need to prepare bedding and wear EC-friendly clothing for more accessible potty breaks. Some parents will remove all pants (nappies and outer clothing) and focus on careful observation. This allows for easy toilet breaks. Split pants are designed for this approach.

Try observation time (without a nappy) after feeding, and observe your baby for any signs of elimination. Keep track of how often your baby eliminates to understand their requirements, and then offer more frequently according to their needs. Always offer before baby naps. By focusing on your baby and their signals, you will become in tune with their communication, and while it may not be evident to others, their signals will become second nature to you.

Bedding and clothing for nappy-free

Bedding Use a woollen or waterproof underlay on the mattress. For quick nighttime bedding changes, layer waterproof and sheeting, so the wet layer is easily removed and a dry layer remains. Don't forget to protect your car seat, buggy/pram and other seating areas with smaller pee-pads.

open-crotch pants by Flappy Nappies. These pants can also be worn with back-up.

Clothing Select clothing that is easy to remove for offering the toilet: T-shirts, stretch pants, night gowns, leg warmers and open-crotch pants. Jeans, coveralls/overalls can be difficult to remove. When your toddler is becoming more independent, it will be important that they can pull up and down their bottom clothing. Zips and buttons can be challenging at this age. Keep it simple, easy to wash and accessible.

Introducing a routine

Newborn babies will do well following a simple routine. By bringing Elimination Communication into your daily routine, your EC journey will be easier. This routine follows natural elimination patterns and is covered in further detail in the newborn section.

1. Feed your baby

2. Remove the nappy, offer toilet opportunity

3. Bare-bum playtime, nappy on once their skin is dry

4. Swaddle baby then back to bed

In addition to this *easy-to-follow routine*, you can offer at *transitional times* and when your *baby signals* the need to eliminate. Over time and closer to toilet independence, the lead will shift from your guidance to your child's independence.

Observation and tracking progress

If you like to track progress, we recommend this free app. Great for caregivers and tracking healthy movements.

 Elimination Communication Log (app by Nyssa Wilfong). Free for Mac and Android users.

- Track pees/poos in the potty, on the way to the potty, or accidents per day
- Track nap time and overnight (dry, wet, poo, both)
- Option to track food and drink by time
- Add daily comments
- View weekly progress
- See your child's pees and poos by time, so you can more easily predict when they'll have to go
- Ability to track for multiple children
- Option to track by time or just daily totals

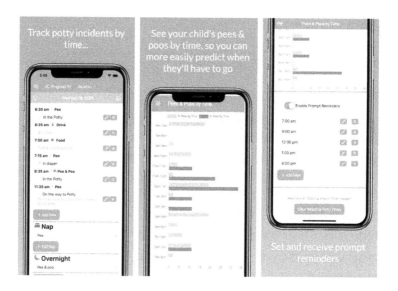

#EliminationCommunicationBabies

A cue for elimination association

Newborns will be familiar with the sound of your voice, and your encouraging voice will be used a lot with each success. For your basic poo and pee cues at toilet practice time, the sound effects of both (raspberries and 'psst psst') are easily understood. Select your own cues for communicating and use them with consistency. Sound association is part of the communication.

Expect things to get messy

Things *will* get messy as you get started, but don't worry... you will get the hang of it. Newborns often have to go toilet while they are feeding as they fill up so quickly. You and your baby will learn together and, with time and practice, you will have success.

Try not to get startled by your explosive little one... their poos are backed by gas and often shoot out with force.

30% of parents choose to EC out of respect for their child[35]

The EC hold

The EC hold is a deep squat supported hold which assists a young baby with elimination. Support baby against your chest and hold under their thighs. The hold should be comfortable for both you and your baby. **Standing:** Try placing an oval bucket in the bathroom sink. The mirror can help with eye contact and communication. The water is convenient for washing up your baby afterwards. **Kneeling:** If you are comfortable with kneeling, a flat-bottom bucket can sit on the floor in front of you. Have a change mat accessible. A toilet can be used once your baby is strong enough. **Sitting:** If you prefer to sit, you can use the toilet by sitting behind your baby for support. See page 70 for photos.

How long in the EC hold?

You will quickly learn how long to hold your baby out to eliminate. Pee is usually quick. You can feel your baby tense up before a poo. If your baby does not need to go, they will probably indicate this as well. You should not be holding out for too long, and if your baby resists, try again next time.

Baby is held out for a short while and will eliminate if they need to

When your baby arrives, you will quickly realise the importance that good sleep has on your own mood, your partner's and your baby as well. Don't forget this. As best as you can, take care of yourself and get ample sleep to help you cope with the demands that parenting a baby brings. Fighting bugs and lack of sleep can bring negative moods. Your energy will be felt by your baby and the household. That goes for everyone's energy!

Consider breastfeeding for the many health benefits it can bring both mother and baby. The cells, hormones and antibodies in breastmilk help protect babies from illness.

Lots of sleep will help the entire family – even if it means sleeping during the day when your baby does. You will be your best when you have your rest!

Stress and pressure

Stay positive. Attitude is everything.

Your energy is running the show, so if you're not coping, stressed or tired, your baby will sense that. Stress can really bugger things up and stop a baby from being relaxed enough. In essence, they clamp up or may opt to use their nappy quietly instead. Highlight this line: *Pressure (in your communication) can cause pushback* – reduce pressure, and in most cases, resistance will reduce. Keep a tab on your levels of expectation and stress. Take advantage of any sleep you can get. Life can be full-on, be kind on yourself.

When will I start?

Depending on your birthing recovery and the health of your newborn, you can get started from birth if you feel comfortable. Your baby is born with instinctual behaviour to be held out and ready for your assistance.

Remember, offering the toilet is not forcing the toilet – just as offering food is not forcing someone to eat. A baby will only eliminate if they need to. You're working this out together, and it is the process around communication that builds trust and establishes a routine baby can rely on. Elimination Communication is a gentle progression toward toilet independence. It's a beautiful and respectful process.

It is important to remember that you will find your own routine with Elimination Communication. Our best advice is to offer consistency and keep it positive!

Now we wait for the safe arrival of your baby.

Join our support group in Facebook: @Elimination Communication Babies Support

Welcome newborn

Section 4 – Welcome newborn

Spend a few days settling in with your new baby and recovering from your birthing experience. What a wonderful time! Some people start at 4 months (after the fourth trimester) but if you and baby are well... let's get started.

First four months – eat, poop, sleep

The newborn months are a special time of bonding and learning for parents and baby. Cherish every moment. The baby is on a liquid diet for the first six months, give or take. Continue with the potty assistance routine and cues.

Consistency and routine are important for babies. Expect lots of little misses as you both settle in. The work you put in now will pay off later.

If you are out and about, you will still be able to offer your baby the opportunity to toilet just as you would at home, and the advantages of not having to clean up a soiled nappy while out and about can make things easier for you.

Hey! I'm Seedy, a relative of Poo. Focus on catching me at this stage. I'll often come after a feed (or during LOL).

Poo and pee – what to expect

Pee

Sticky

#1stPoo

Expect to change at least six to eight wet nappies a day if breastfeeding and up to 10 if formula-feeding, as formula-fed babies will take in more fluid than a breastfed baby.

All babies differ, so there is a range in bowel movement numbers. You might like to keep track of your baby's pee and poo times to ensure your baby is thriving. We recommend the *Elimination Communication Log* app.

Baby's first sticky black poo is called meconium. It will pass within the first few days. It's made up of mucus, amniotic fluid, and everything your baby has ingested while in your uterus (womb). Meconium indicates that the baby's digestive system is working normally.

Your first thick yellow milk is called colostrum. It helps protect your baby against infection and acts as a laxative that pushes the meconium through. Once your milk comes in – about three days after you give birth – your baby's poos will gradually change.

Seedy

#SquirtyBum

Next comes a sweet-smelling stool with a seedy mustard appearance, which will vary in look and odour depending on whether baby is breastfed or bottle-fed. Your baby's poo should become lighter over time, starting out green-brown and becoming bright and mustard yellow. Because of the texture, it is often confused with diarrhoea.

Breastfed babies' bowel movements vary widely. Some babies infrequently poo while others poo after each feed. It also varies with bottle-fed babies, but typically they poo more frequently. Again, their poo will vary in colour from pale yellow to yellowish-brown. As formula is not fully digested, bottle-fed babies can be prone to constipation, and their poo consistency could be thicker and stronger smelling.

Reasons to call your medical adviser:

- The baby's stool contains whitish mucus.

- The baby's stool contains streaks or flecks of red.

- Suspected constipation.

Be the unicorn in the field of horses.

#EliminationCommunicationBabies

When you are ready and confident to hold your baby in a supported squat, it's a good time to introduce your toilet routine. You will be pleasantly surprised to see how quickly your baby will eliminate if you start in the newborn stage. Newborns have a small bladder; therefore, they pee a lot. Don't worry about catching every pee. You're just getting into the swing of this, and it's all about the process and communication.

Elimination Communication hold positions support baby beneath the thigh area with their neck and head resting on you. The position puts your baby into a squat, making it easy for them to eliminate. Neither you nor your baby should feel uncomfortable.

Hi, I'm Pee. Don't worry about me too much at this stage. I'll be here often! In the potty and inbetween...

Ensure baby is well supported and that you are in a comfortable position.

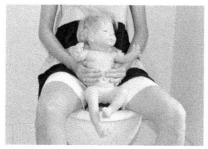
Sitting behind baby on the toilet.

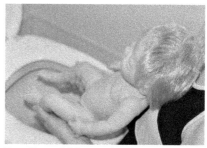
Kneeling, child can also face you when they are bigger.

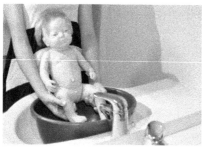
Standing – use of a bathroom sink. The mirror is great for baby, and the tap is handy for clean-up.

Football hold – baby is held resting on one arm.

Top hat potty, or any container that you can hold like this old potty.

Floor kneel – flat-bottom bucket.

Newborn babies will do well following a simple routine:

1. **Feed your baby** after waking. Burp your baby well to ensure there is no wind after feeding. Sometimes babies may start elimination during a feed, in which case you can hold a small potty beneath them or break a feed into two.

2. **Remove the nappy, offer toilet opportunity.** This can take care of gas build-up.
   - Use cues to let baby know it's toilet time while in position over a potty.
   - Use your encouraging voice when you have success.
   - Clean baby with warm water and a mild soap (rather than disposable wipes).

3. **Bare-bum playtime** on a change mat. Tummy time (**peach time**) and back time to have a kick. Engage baby with smiles and talk or song. When dry and ready, put the nappy back on. Baby is generally awake only 45 minutes or so before becoming tired again.

1. Eat
2. Toilet
3. Play
4. Sleep

4. Swaddle your baby then **back to bed** in a warm dark room when you notice your baby is tired.

Tip

Print this page out and really learn this simple routine.

71

Offering at transitions and when baby signals are in addition to the routine based around natural elimination rhythms. When you notice a signal from your baby, this is your best time to respond if possible. Elimination signals can be tricky to detect, so offering routinely will establish the practice.

Newborns are typically not awake for long periods, but you will have more 'awake' time for toilet assistance as they get older. Paying close attention to baby while they are without a nappy can help you learn their elimination signals but don't get stuck here. Transitional times could look like:

- Upon waking (or wait until after the first feed)
- Before sleeping (can lead to dry naps over time)
- Before a bath
- Exiting a baby carrier
- Before and after vehicle trips (car/car seats).

This may seem like a lot, and we don't want to 'overdo it'. Once you learn your baby's elimination patterns and establish a rhythm with your baby, you will be in tune with their elimination needs, and it won't feel overwhelming. It's a real benefit when you get to the stage of knowing when your baby will most likely need to poo so that you won't be caught out.

Happiness is enjoying the little things in life!

Remove the baby's nappy and offer the opportunity to eliminate. Ensure baby is warm and fed first.

Choose one of the positions to hold your baby over a potty. Ensure that baby's head and neck are well supported. Make a cue sound, whistle or use a word. An obvious cue for a pee is a psst-psst noise. An obvious cue for a poo is 'blowing a raspberry' (poke out tongue and rattle it). Blowing a raspberry, strawberry or making a Bronx cheer makes a noise similar to flatulence. Running water can also trigger pee. If your baby is not comfortable or is upset, try again later.

Babies on a change mat (without a nappy) will often eliminate when exposed to the cold air, so things should flow naturally for them. Offering your baby an opportunity to eliminate after each feed will ensure they have regular opportunities. Newborns don't hold on when they need to go and have small bladders and frequently pee, so don't worry about catching every pee. What they are learning is a consistent pattern around elimination and a natural and healthy way to eliminate.

Nighttime elimination 0–4 months

If you're keen to try nighttime Elimination Communication, here is an overview for the 0–4 month stage. Sleep is super important and very broken during this time. When your baby wakes during the night, find the right time to offer the potty (before a feed, during or afterwards), then settle back to sleep. Elimination opportunities are also provided before bed and upon wake-up.

If you're not ready to try it, no stress; ensure baby is in good quality absorbent nappies to get through the night, or they may require a quick change during the night if feeding a lot. Offer before bed and either upon waking or after the first morning feed with the morning nappy change.

Here are tips if you are offering during the night. Keep a potty in the room handy. The bedding should have a waterproof underlay. Night lights or a salt lamp can provide enough gentle lighting to help you. Keep the room dim and warm, and the pee opportunity should take no longer than a minute, so they are not disturbed from sleep too much. Breastfeeding can be advantageous during the night for the same reason because your baby won't need to wait long. If it is taking longer and disturbs sleep, think about if it is worth pursuing at this stage.

When a baby wriggles or grizzles during the night, you can try offering the potty, then settle your baby back to sleep with a feed. A top hat style potty works well for a dream pee. Even if a baby is sleepy, they will usually pee on cue. The cue association is essential, and they will easily pee on cue when half asleep.

Generally, babies eliminate when awake or in a light sleep state, so a grizzle is often a signal they are awake or about to eliminate. Most babies won't poo during the night, although some will poo upon waking up and often after their

#EliminationCommunicationBabies

first feed. Some people will drop nappies at night before dropping nappies during the day.

Your baby's communication 0–4 months

During this stage, your baby communicates with verbal noises, facial expressions and body language. Eye contact and body contact (being held) is very important. You may notice the following natural signals when baby needs to eliminate – pulling off at feeding, glassy eyes, passing gas, smiles, grizzles, grunts, discomfort noises, shivering, general fussing, wriggling, tightening, stiffening, crying, squirming, straining, grimacing, vocalising, intent look at caregiver or a red face.

Starting EC during the first four months

The first four months is an easy time to establish a toilet routine with your baby. Introducing the concept of being held out to eliminate, or assisted while sitting on a potty will be a new experience for your baby. Start with the routine outlined in this section, taking note of baby's signals. Your baby may need to be transitioned from eliminating in a nappy. If this is the case, begin to introduce your cues to your baby to eliminate when you notice baby is using their nappy. After sound association, remove the nappy and continue. Move quickly into offering based on timing and routine. At this age and with consistent assistance, your baby will adapt well to potty use.

> What you do not want done to yourself, do not do to others.
> Confucius

Dealing with change

Babies are adaptable, so keep your emotions calm, and any change or life upsets should not trouble your baby with their Elimination Communication at this stage. Keep consistently offering toilet opportunities – this routine can provide your baby with a sense of stability when other things in life are not the same as usual. Babies thrive on routine.

If you are positive you will see opportunities instead of obstacles.

Introducing a caregiver to EC

Any caregiver can assist with Elimination Communication. If you have already established a successful routine with your baby, it will be easier for your caregiver to assist your baby. The caregiver can then provide your baby with the routine they are familiar with. At this age, the adult to baby ratio in care is low. Offering the baby a toilet opportunity does not take much longer than a nappy change. It is important at this age to continue allowing baby time to dry (bare-bottom time) after their elimination if this is possible in care. It is helpful to understand when your baby is offered the toilet or when they pass stool. Most care providers will record these details as part of their service. The *Elimination Communication Log* app is an excellent tool for sharing this information.

If you're out and about a lot with your baby, you may wonder how to offer the toilet when you are not at home. Parents are resourceful, and you will find a way to assist your baby most times when you are away from home.

With very young babies, it can help to plan your trips around your feeding times, so you can account for a comfortable place to feed and a good facility to potty and change them. Some people are very uncomfortable in public washroom facilities. Try not to express this discomfort around your baby. Exposing your baby to different toilet situations is good practice. Here are some scenarios and how you might EC with a baby on a liquid diet.

Nature – Bushwalks and green areas or beachside, babies can be 'held out' away from people where you can wash away any liquid waste with a water bottle. Small potties can be helpful in the vehicle or outdoors, and some containers with lids are ideal for containing waste. Try to remember to offer the potty before vehicle trips and upon arrival if you are travelling some distance.

Shopping or baby classes
– Parenting rooms offer good privacy where a baby can be held out over a toilet or where you would sit behind your baby. If there is a private sink, you could place a nappy/insert or paper towel in a

Babies are born ready to potty! They just need help like they do with feeding too.

sink to catch waste. Disposable wipes are useful for these situations but never flush these – place in the nappy bins provided.

Friends and relatives – You should feel comfortable feeding and toileting your baby in another home; however, EC is not commonly understood, so you may experience questions. Be confident in your approach. If you have your own travel potty, it will be easy and familiar to use.

Air travel – Typically, long-haul is not recommended before age 3 months old. Airport facilities are easier to use than toilets onboard the plane, so offer before and when you exit the plane. On long haul flights, you will inevitably require the facilities. Facilities can become very messy onboard – and the space inside the facility is very tight. There is generally a fold-down change table above the toilet. Line this with your own portable or disposable change mat. Often with air travel, babies and children will naturally hold on to their stool. Don't stress, do your best to keep baby dry and hydrated and worry about the routine at your destination if it is too tricky onboard. Tip: Don't overfeed baby on a plane to avoid spill and blowout. Feed or offer a dummy at take-off and landing. It can help with air pressure.

For seat hygiene in public toilets, you can purchase products such as spray on and wipe off sanitizers, wipes and paper seat liners.

Between 1 and 4 months:

- Beginning to follow cues at toilet time.

Milestone concerns

Every baby develops at a different rate, however, don't hesitate to have baby checked by your doctor when you notice the following:

- Baby does not respond to loud sounds.

- Baby feeds very slowly or does not suck well.

- Baby does not react to bright lights.

- Baby seems stiff or floppy.

- Baby does not seem to focus well or notice moving things.

Elimination Communication won't go so well if your baby is struggling with something – a healthy baby and a healthy parent are always the first priority.

If your baby has poop issues (loose or hard), make an appointment with an allergist, even if you are breastfeeding.

Stay positive, realise all babies are different, so don't make any comparisons to others.

Tips 0–4 months

- Always wash away urine from your baby's skin and offer a time on the change mat to dry, to avoid rash.

- Ensure baby is warm and fed before offering the potty. Baby may fuss if cold or hungry.

- Follow our basic Eat, Toilet, Play, Sleep routine to avoid blow-outs and rash, and allow your baby time to wriggle on the change mat, on the floor.

- Newborn baby skin is delicate. Use olive oil around the groin area to moisturise if necessary.

- Expect accidents. When your baby is exposed to cold air, it is common for them to wet themselves. Have their potty handy.

- Once you both become familiar with toilet practice, your baby will learn when and where to go and cleaning up becomes much easier.

Elimination
Communication
I watch and listen for your needs. I'm proactive and respond.

- Potty clean-up is easy too. It can be rinsed into the toilet and will not leave any bad smells in your house.

- If your baby suffers from gas, place your baby on their back and move their legs in bicycle movements to help alleviate any pain and gas build-up. Movement will help get other things moving. Place baby on your arm or leg, face down, and rock gently to move baby. Elimination Communication can be a relief for colic.[36]

- Even before baby is on solid food, they may experience allergies through breast milk or formula. If their stool becomes hard or soft, it could be worth getting an allergy test.

"When we were planning to have our third child, we made a conscious decision to not use disposable nappies. We felt sheepish that we had already contributed 2 children's worth of nappies to our nation's landfills." …

"During those first weeks of life, we regularly attempted toilet time at awakening and after each feed accompanied with a short whistle. This was often followed by her naturally relieving herself. By the end of 1 month, we were only having 1 to 2 'misses' per day." …

"Our worthwhile experience with EC compels us to offer our perspective as working parents and physicians. We strongly feel that this underrecognised approach to toilet training could be beneficial to US families in terms of child health, convenience, and expense. It further helps Americans struggling to protect the environment for our children and generations to come." …

"Providers who care for children should learn more about EC and incorporate this alternative into their discussions with young and growing families." [37]

Quotes from Dr Bender (Paediatric Infectious Specialist) and Dr She (Pathologist and Medical Microbiologist), parents of three children from Los Angeles, California who offered Elimination Communication to their third child.

Solid work.
4–8 months

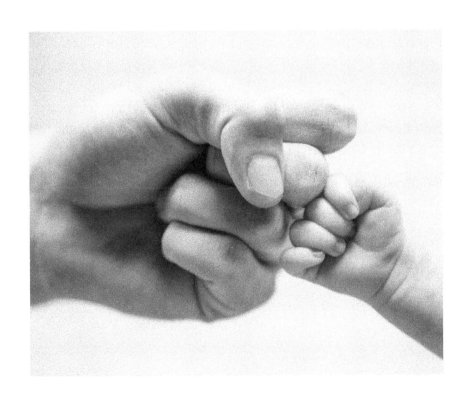

Section 5 – Solid work. 4–8 months

You are doing so well. Keep up the amazing work. You've come so far already, even if it may not feel like it. You have established routines and spent a whole lot of time bonding with your little one. Most of your learning has happened in the first four months, and as your baby grows and develops, you will continue to learn and adjust.

During the next four months, most babies will learn how to sit and will start solid foods. Active babies may also begin to crawl and pull up to stand at furniture. It's time to plan for your baby's next developments. What a journey... let's keep going.

If you're just getting started at this stage, welcome – it's a great age to get started. Baby will soon transition from a liquid diet to solids, and the evident solids that result in that! It's a perfect time to get that sorted and landing in the potty! Read over the previous sections, as much of this will still apply at this stage.

What you will need:

- A small floor potty.

- A cleaning brush/cleaner (for potty care).

- Small toys and simple books.

- A watchful eye and a positive mindset.

Hey! I'll be making my debut soon... right after some solid food. Potty me please! I don't want to mess up my solid style.

Daytime routine 4–8 months

Keep up your consistent routine by offering your baby the chance to eliminate after food and if you notice an elimination signal from your baby. Baby should now be more settled with day sleep and feeding patterns, and you will find that offering at transitional times will also become more manageable.

We recommend using the proper toilet or a floor potty by the time your baby starts solid food. Your baby will also become too heavy for an EC hold. You can start to use regular toilet paper when your baby's poo becomes solid as well.

Potty time will continue to be a social time for you and your baby. A time to talk, discover a few small toys or books or learn some baby sign language. Keep ensuring your baby is well dry before putting the nappy back on. As your baby becomes more mobile, be mindful of additional spillage if you've not put the nappy back on. Explain why we use a potty and keep it positive.

Nighttime routine 4–8 months

You may notice sleep regression during baby's fourth month, but sleep will generally start to settle into longer periods during these four months.

If you have decided to offer the potty during the nighttime, continue as you have been, keeping the offer timing to under a minute if possible. Notice baby's movements and night noises for their

1. Eat
2. Toilet
3. Play
4. Sleep

awake periods and offer a dream pee (or change of nappy if necessary) before resettling back to sleep. You may try to offer a top hat style potty while feeding to resettle. By keeping the room dimly lit and being efficient with your assistance, sleep can resume quickly. A nightgown covering a nappy will allow for more accessible toileting. Where possible, let baby sleep and catch your rest as well. No one functions well on a lack of sleep. Once your baby is eventually sleeping through the night, your first toilet opportunity will be in the morning. If you have a heavy wetter, you may need to offer a couple of times during the night, for example, 10 pm and 2 am – or roughly every four hours. Offer the toilet before baby naps during the daytime as well. However, don't offer during a daytime nap, as this will wake the baby, and they most likely won't resettle.

Your baby's communication

Your baby will form verbal sounds and understand emotions and basic words, so communicating with your baby is very important. You could try introducing some baby sign language or another non-verbal toilet cue during this time. Continue to watch your baby for the natural elimination

signals during these ages. Keep a watchful eye for any indication they are trying to communicate elimination needs with you.

Using baby sign language.

Welcome to the Elimination Communication journey. Your baby has become accustomed to eliminating in the nappy but it will be easy to transition to a potty during this age range. Around this time, your baby will be able to sit assisted and then unassisted on a potty. If your baby is still tiny, an EC hold may work better for you (review the newborn stage). Introduce sitting on the potty as part of your daily routine (see page 71), while talking about what you are doing and why. You can also introduce hand signals such as baby sign language at the same time. Your baby will benefit from watching you or a sibling use the toilet. Some babies will appreciate something to hold or play with while sitting. Provide your complete attention during potty time to engage with your baby. Take your time and explore different toilet options (potty, seat reducer) until your baby is happy. Try to make it a positive and relaxed process, and don't expect too much. If your baby resists, try at the next opportunity. Keep offering and be confident in what you are doing. Keep on communicating with your baby and engage their communication. Making it part of their normal daily routine is what you are aiming to do.

Potty 4–8 months

Switching from an EC hold to a potty can be done by using your cues. You may keep your hands beneath your baby's thighs in a hold while sitting on the potty to begin with if the transition requires it.

Introduce baby to the potty right after a meal. Provide some small toys for your baby to explore while sitting. Never leave baby alone on the potty. Always place the potty on the floor, never on a bench or at height. Stay close, talk to your baby and offer encouragement while you are giving the cues. Some older babies will launch off the potty right after they are done, so watch out for:

- Spillage from the potty.

- Baby exploring the potty contents.

- Baby 'posting' toys into the potty.

If your baby is quite active, you may notice the potty becomes a vehicle for sliding around the room. Watch out for obstacles. Once your baby is done and cleaned off, continue to offer bare-bottom time. Flush away the potty contents and clean the potty for next time.

Big toilet 4–8 months

Introduce baby to the big toilet by sitting directly behind baby in a supportive position or holding securely and use your familiar cues. When a baby can sit independently, you can sit them onto a toilet with a seat reducer facing you, but give them some support. Babies with older siblings might prefer the big toilet, as that is what their siblings use.

A baby is born with a need to be loved – and never grows out of it.
Frank Clark

Once your baby is familiar with the toilet, outings are much more manageable; however, you can still pack a small potty if you prefer. The potty is still more common at this age.

Cues 4–8 months

Keep offering baby the same cues, along with conversation. You may find baby understands without the sound cue now. Your baby may even start to imitate your sound cues. If you are using baby sign language, you may choose to introduce the sign for the toilet, which is placing your thumb between your first two fingers and shaking your fist. Don't expect your baby to tell you they need to go just yet. Keep up the communication and be observant. Baby is always learning.

Oopsies or misses

Some babies will decide on a new 'potty' place, such as an exersaucer or the highchair. Remember to use your encouraging voice when you get success on the proper potty. If you notice your baby in the act of going, sometimes they can finish their business on the floor potty. Talk to your baby and remind them gently to use the potty rather than their nappy (or elsewhere). They do understand.

When your baby is in the highchair, you may notice they are not interested in eating or become fidgety. This is a natural signal that your baby needs to 'go' potty. Often while eating, they can very quickly become full and need to go. You may find you need to offer the potty before the main meal or partway through. Stay positive; your baby will get back on track with consistency and positive encouragement. Everything is an opportunity to learn, so it is all positive progress. Having the potty nearby can be helpful during this stage.

Dealing with change 4–8 months

You may find yourself in a big life-changing situation or even a small routine change such as a vacation. Despite the changes, if you have a solid routine, your baby will find comfort in knowing what comes next. Developmental change can also affect your baby. Regardless of what is going on, keep offering the toilet routinely – even if the output has stalled. Keep this a constant, reliable thing in their life.

Introducing a caregiver to EC

If your baby is going into care (at any age), it's important to choose a provider that offers you support and offers your baby similar consistency around elimination that you offer your baby at home. It could be confusing for your baby if elimination practices are not consistent.

All centres should accommodate; however, some of the larger centres change nappies at set times, which may not align well with this approach. When you are interviewing providers, ask them specifically about their nappy change routines and how they would accommodate your baby with the toilet. Explain what you have been doing at home. Home-based providers or nannies will easily be able to offer the same elimination consistency.

When your baby first starts care, and with any significant change, they will most likely have toilet-practice setbacks. Don't worry. With consistency and encouragement, your baby will get back on track. Other changes that may cause setbacks could include a new baby in the family, moving house, or family stress.

Ask the caregiver to provide the toilet after meals and before a nap to avoid guesswork. Daycares often have special tiny toilets installed. You may need to provide a potty for your child. Care providers often chart progress. We recommend the *Elimination Communication Log* app to share this data with you.

Out and about 4–8 months

Going out gets easier once your baby is more settled with sleep and feeding. Once your baby can sit and eat solid food, using a toilet or potty when out of the home gets easier also.

Potty station in the vehicle – It's a good idea to offer the potty before a trip and upon arrival if possible. Some people like to keep a potty in the back of their vehicle. This is ideal when a toilet stop is required and there is no restroom convenient. A lidded potty or travel potty with waste bags is a good idea for this scenario. A roll of dog poop bags could come in handy for used wipes.

Nature – If you plan a day trip into nature, you will need to accommodate the baby by taking a potty along if you don't think the facilities will be suitable. Don't stray too far from a washroom or a suitable place to toilet unless you are going into a remote area, in which case bury or collect the waste as you would for a puppy. Rinse or wipe the potty and hike on.

Family and friends – Do as you do at home. If you feel uncomfortable explaining what you are doing and why, you don't need to explain. You'll find the right time to share EC, and we're always happy to hear how you are getting on. Always take home anything that might leave a smell unless you're welcome to leave it behind. Your friends and family may well fully support EC or get a thrill to see that it works.

Shopping or baby classes – Public washrooms with parenting rooms or a larger stall that fits a buggy/pram are ideal. It can be a little tricky, especially if you are by yourself with your baby and need the washroom as well. In some instances, you'll need to leave a buggy, and strap baby to a change table. If you have been practicing using a big toilet with your baby, you won't have too much trouble in public washrooms.

Travel – Travel can involve public washrooms and onboard washrooms. As discussed in the previous stage, when travelling a child does sometimes hold stool back, although this is not always the case. Try to treat the routine the same as you would at home by offering after eating. Elimination Communication will give your baby confidence to potty in a variety of places. Be confident, and treat it as you would for yourself – a natural and normal part of the day.

Milestones 4–8 months

- Change in stool as a result of solid food.

- Beginning to sit on the potty.

- Understanding the cues for toilet practice. May imitate your cues.

- Showing a consistent pattern in elimination.

- Just starting to learn self-control.

Tips 4–8 months

- Get your partner involved with your baby's toilet practice so that everyone is comfortable and supportive.

- Starting solid foods is an exciting step but could also bring food intolerances or allergies. Introduce one food at a time and be watchful for any reactions. Learn which foods are safest to start with and learn which foods to avoid for now. Notice the change in stool consistency. Allergies can mess up potty time if they cause constipation. Seek medical advice regarding allergies if necessary.

- Watch out for constipation when introducing solid foods and seek medical advice if necessary.

- Watch out for diarrhoea. Gastrointestinal infections, colds, food intolerances or food allergies, and antibiotics are common causes. Seek medical advice if necessary.

- Use both the potty and big toilet so that outings are easier.

- Keep a potty handy in case you need to use it quickly. It can be convenient to have more than one potty in the house.

- Don't use a complicated potty that is bulky or difficult to clean. A small one-piece potty is the easiest to clean.

Watch me for natural and intentional signals that I need to eliminate.

Busy baby.
9–12 months

Slow down, baby; this is going too fast! No, seriously, "Slow down!" Your little one will be on the move already or will be soon, so here we enter a new stage and suddenly have to grow eyes on the back of our head. Keeping your baby safe while they explore their world is essential at this stage. Be watchful of small objects and hazards around the home. You are heading toward the first-year milestone in this stretch. Keep up the great work!

If you're learning about Elimination Communication now, that's awesome – it's not too late to start. Read back through the other stages to catch up.

What you will need:

○ A simple one-piece potty.

○ A seat reducer. Your baby may also be ready for the big toilet by now. Some will require a seat reducer.

○ A cleaning brush/cleaner (for potty care).

○ Small toys and books.

○ A step-stool for the bathroom.

○ To be positive and supportive.

Positive mind. Positive vibes. Positive life.

9–12 months. Go, go …oh!

Now that your baby is most likely mobile, this brings new challenges with the toilet.

Does your baby like to sit for some time on the potty? Perhaps they jump off as soon as they have done their business? Be extra vigilant at this stage and pay attention to the potty as its contents may become a place of discovery. Your baby may put their hands in it, poke objects into it, or tip it over... oh! It's a little like the shape posting game! Small books and toys might help to keep your little one amused while they sit. If your baby often leaps off the potty, tipping it over, you could try placing the potty and your little one in an empty bathtub or use a waterproof mat beneath the potty if necessary. Never leave your baby alone while using the potty. Some babies like to scoot around the room on their potty like a mini car; be mindful of hazards.

Take a mental note of how often your little one does their business. Have you noticed a pattern by now? It is healthy to fall into a regular routine with poo and pass at least once a day. After eating a meal is a typical time to eliminate – one meal in, one meal out! Knowing their pattern will help you anticipate these movements so that you can offer the potty at an appropriate time.

Don't judge each day by the harvest you reap, but by the seeds that you plant.
R. Stevenson

For example, your big eater might do a poo right after lunch and then again after dinner.

Keep offering routinely and keep a watchful eye for your baby communicating with you, especially around the times you offer. Encourage your baby to tell you with a signal. A tap on the thigh or baby sign language are easy non-verbal signs they can learn.

Once your baby can balance, stand and walk (this may be after 12 months), you can help them learn to get on and off the potty independently.

Nighttime routine 9–12 months

Hopefully, by now, you are getting better sleep at night. Night lights will be helpful to have in your baby's room and on the way to the bathroom at this stage. Offer the potty before your baby's bedtime. Next, offer a dream pee to your baby when you are going to bed. If your baby stirs during the night, this can indicate their need to eliminate again. Their liquid intake during the night will affect how much they pee. Some parents will choose to offer again before the morning, offering approximately every three to four hours. Some babies may drop nappies altogether at night around this time, in some cases before dropping daytime nappies.

Keep a waterproof or wool layer beneath the sheeting, just in case. You can layer sheets with waterproofing layers for a quick nighttime bed change. In the morning, offer upon waking and again after their first feeding. If you're not offering during the night, then offer at bedtime and then upon waking up. However, you might need to change their nappy during the night to avoid a leaky nappy.

As your little one is getting bigger, there will come a time when they can manage sitting on the big toilet. At this time, you can introduce the toilet seat insert/seat reducer.

Let your little person watch you using the toilet. They learn by observing, so don't be shy. Children with older siblings will learn by watching them and will pick this up very quickly as they will naturally want to be doing just the same as their older siblings.

You can carefully sit your little one on the seat, so they are facing you while you crouch down and support them. Make eye contact, and encourage them as this will help them feel safe.

Your baby might not yet be ready for the toilet during this stage, but keep the toilet in mind. If your little one begins to resist the potty, trying the toilet can be an exciting development for them. They may be mentally ready to progress but can't verbalise it yet. Always keep toilet time positive – even when you are out using a public toilet. Try not to create any negative association about using the toilet.

Show your little one how the toilet flushes. If they are using the potty still, they may want to help tip the contents into the toilet. Say "Bye-bye" to their business. They will get enjoyment from watching and helping. But remember to close the lid afterwards. Your little one loves to explore and can probably reach into the bowl by now – it's fun for them to post objects like your phone or entire rolls of paper.

Learning your baby's signals

Watch for signs that your little one needs to go. You will know your baby and learn their signals. Here are some examples:

- While in the highchair, they may stop eating if they need to poo.

- They may lean slightly forward or become agitated or wriggle in their seat.

- Breaking wind is a good indication they need to go. A grunt or a push means they are about to start! Ask them to hold on until you can move to the potty to finish off.

- Eye contact, glassy eyes, a shiver or a distant stare.

- Watch for any deliberate signals you have taught them, such as baby sign language.

Comprehension

At this age, you will be noticing signs that your baby's comprehension is very good. For example, you may say "Goodbye" and baby waves. You may ask, "Where is the banana?" and your baby points. Now is a great time to use baby sign language more frequently. Try the 'toilet' sign and

BE consistent and **DO** what it takes to **HAVE** what you want

the 'all done' sign. You can also ask your baby to wait for the potty.

There are fantastic videos online to learn sign language. If you see your baby showing signals they need to go while in the highchair, for example, you can ask them to "wait until you go in the potty – we can go to the potty now".

Your baby will understand the use of the potty by now. Comprehension is improved by your conversations with them and reading with them. Give them lots of your attention, and explain your daily routines to them. Even if they don't understand every word, they will be learning so much through the dialogue.

Setbacks

Resistance can start with independence, and around 12 months it can be a common time to experience some pushback. You may also notice resistance toward some food options or at bedtime. Just remember, it is normal, and it is a stage that will pass. It is also an important stage, as your baby is expressing their independence.

Here are some tips you can try if you experience resistance:

- Try using the big toilet if resistance is with the potty. They may want to progress.

- In a matter-of-fact and positive statement, you can remind your baby that you are very happy when they use the potty.

- Give your full attention while they potty, offer small toys or books (rotate toys to keep them fresh, just for potty time). Engage in conversation.

- Try role-playing with a toy.

- Reduce offering to the basics. You may be over-offering. Try cutting back to just the basics. Check in with yourself – if you are stressed, it won't be helping them.

- If they are arching their back or straightening legs and really acting out, try another time and never force it. Don't stop offering opportunities altogether; try again at another time. They may be tired.

Any number of reasons can also contribute toward pushback. Feeling off, teething or bad sleep are some examples. Stay positive and confident in what you are doing. Offering is not forcing and each day is another chance to try again.

With soiled nappies, stay neutral when cleaning up your baby. If you feel your baby may need to keep going, offer the chance to sit on the potty. If they refuse, it's OK. Remind them you are happy when they go on the potty. Explaining the benefits of using the potty in a matter-of-fact way can also be helpful: "Next time, let's use the potty as it is easier to clean you up", for example.

Sleep, sickness and well-being

Take care of your mental well being with good sleep. Broken sleep or not enough sleep can increase parents, and children's negative moods (anger, frustration, irritability, sadness). If you are feeling run down or fighting a bug, your mood may also be affected. If you find yourself getting frustrated or anxious, you need to step back. Take a break or reduce offering to the basics – after waking, before naps and after eating. Bringing stress into this space can affect the way the child responds. We don't want any toilet anxiety. Likewise, if your baby is run down or tired, keep it to a minimum or take a pause. There is no pressure or deadline to meet, and tomorrow is always another day.

Role-play

Later in this stage, you may notice your little one placing their doll or toy onto the potty before they go (or after – in which case, watch out, teddy bear!). This is great role-playing in action. You can encourage role-play if your baby is showing signs of resistance.

Starting EC from 9–12 months

We're so glad you are joining us! Start by reading the previous sections. Assuming you are just getting started and have not done any potty assistance prior, your baby will be established using the nappy for elimination. Changing this habit can be successful at this age and will require commitment and consistency. Your baby will have good comprehension by this age. Talk with your baby about the new place to go toilet. Start to introduce signals they can use and sound association for pee and poo. Initiate role-play and let your baby observe you or family members using the toilet.

You may already have a good sense for when your little one eliminates. Removing the nappy for some time after eating can help you observe their signals before they eliminate, however as they are now on the move this can be a messy experience. If you do happen to see your baby using their nappy, mention what you are observing and take your baby to the potty. Remove the nappy and sit baby on the potty. They may be finished, but work on this association with elimination. Keep this positive. Your baby may have a 'spot' where they poo, such as behind a couch. Place a potty in this location, and use this location to start introducing the potty. During this time, you will still use a nappy as back-up.

If you start by proactively offering the potty or toilet after each snack or meal with your cues, your baby will learn what to do. Introducing the potty or toilet as part of the normal daily routine is what you are aiming for. Don't worry about every pee at this stage. We will want the focus to be on poo to start. You may need to keep the nappy off after each meal until they

Play gives children a chance to practice what they are learning.
Mr. Rogers

have used the potty. This is not so they can walk around and pee everywhere – you will need to keep the potty close by; perhaps set up a few toys in the bathroom and then guide them to sit on the potty when they are showing signs. Don't expect them to work this out on their own. This is a new process for your baby, and you will need to guide, encourage and be there to assist and be consistent with this. This does pay off; be positive in what you are doing.

Dealing with change 9–12 months

Change and development can both contribute to potty resistance or setbacks. While this is happening, it's important to try to keep offering the opportunities to eliminate. If there are other changes in their world, this routine can be helpful as it gives your baby a sense of understanding their world and what is coming next. Keeping their life as normal as possible during periods of change will keep them feeling secure.

Illness can be a messy time and a cause for setbacks. Health is your priority. The potty can take a rest and be picked up when the baby is well. You may notice a setback, but with consistency, you will get back on track again.

> Change is hard at first, messy in the middle and gorgeous at the end.
> R. Sharma

Introducing a caregiver to EC

If you have been doing Elimination Communication for some time, your routine will be well established by now. Introducing a new person to help with the toilet at home can be helpful for the transition into care. A parent or friend can help. When you interview care providers, ask them if they will assist with your baby's potty or toilet and explain what you do at home.

When your baby starts at the new centre, take the baby to the new washroom to help them settle in. This is important, as they may appreciate privacy, and a new toilet can sometimes cause anxiety (and result in holding on). If your baby has had the opportunity to use many different toilets, this can help alleviate any concerns over a new toilet situation. Bringing along a familiar potty to their centre can help.

Explain your routine to the care provider. At the very least, if the potty is provided after snacks and meals, your baby should not have any setbacks. You can also offer it at the centre before going home.

Out and about 9–12 months

Getting out and about is getting easier. Just as you would provide snacks, be prepared to offer the toilet when you are out; as mentioned above, using unfamiliar toilets will help your little one become comfortable with this very normal daily need. If you have any personal hang-ups with public toilets, please try not to project these onto your baby. Pack a potty or if you are comfortable, use the big toilet with a seat reducer if this makes baby feel comfortable. It becomes easy when you know their elimination patterns. Be as easygoing as possible with the toilet when you are out and about.

Parenting rooms are convenient and usually offer good facilities and room for a parent and baby in one stall. They are often big enough to fit your buggy, which is helpful when you need to use the facilities. If you don't have this option, take your baby with you into the gender room you use. Don't fret if they touch surfaces – hands are washed at the end. Try to keep toilet experiences neutral or positive. Never flush wipes and remember these spaces are shared, so clean up any mess your little one makes for the next person. Experiences in public facilities all provide good learning for your baby.

This section is similar to the previous stage; refer back to page 91.

Milestones 9–12 months

- Is comfortable using the potty/toilet in a variety of places.

- Beginning to show signs of communicating, e.g. nods for 'Yes' and 'No'.

- Could be showing interest in the big toilet.

- Is learning about self-control.

- Lots of positive encouragement at this age will help.

- Don't be fazed by setbacks. Work with your little one to encourage them back on track. Never push or force, and this goes for toilet training as well.

- Have lots of wipe-up cloth handy for spills.

- Pay lots of attention to your little one while they are on the toilet. Sing little songs, read stories and talk.

- They should not have to strain too much when eliminating. Be watchful of constipation especially with new foods.

Wow, did you just fart? Because you totally blew me away!

...

Remember to observe with all your senses!

Toward toilet independence.
12 months+

Section 7 – Toward toilet independence. 12 months+

From age 1 onward, you and your toddler are well on your way and may no longer be experiencing stool in nappies. Wahoo! By now, you may be moving into trainer underwear or pull-ups. As every child is different, the tips to reach toilet independence will apply to you when your child is showing signs of dryness. In some cases, this is before 12 months. Typically, toilet independence occurs sometime after they are walking. Be patient and consistent. It will happen, but don't rush the process.

You're entering a stage where your toddler is becoming more independent, which is an important step. You will reach a time where a shift happens from your direction to your child's self-direction. Your guidance will still be necessary as they reach toilet independence. It may not feel like it yet, but you're nearly there. Keep positive and carry on.

Don't be put off if you experience some setbacks or power struggles. This is the most common age/stage for resistance. This can happen when they want more control or for a variety of other reasons. We can work with this – let's keep going.

You will reach your goal by taking baby steps each day.

#EliminationCommunicationBabies

What you will need:

○   Absorbent training underwear, then underwear.

○   Waterproof mattress cover for bedding.

○   Waterproof 'pee pads' for your pushchair and car seat.

○   Night lights.

○   A *lot* of excitement.

12 months+

Happy first birthday to your super little one, and congratulations to you for an amazing first year. What a fantastic learning journey; think about how far you have come. During this stage, you will transition to using the toilet (if you have not already been using it). Your toddler will start walking (if not already), and we will be moving into pull-ups/ training pants and finally underwear. There will be so many firsts to celebrate and share!

Yes, I am totally ONE-derful!

Daytime routine 12 months+

From 12 months onwards you will continue to offer the toilet after each meal while also keeping a watch for their communication back to you. Around this age, they can crawl to and point to the potty. They may also have started to use simple words. Keep a potty visible for them.

Keep offering at transitional times as well. Is your toddler regular with poo? If your child is in care, check to see if they did a poo while in care each day. Passing at least one poo a day is healthy. They often wait until they are home, where they are more relaxed. Often after dinner is a typical time to poop.

Ensure enough time at the start or end of the day in your home for your toddler to poo comfortably at home. As you progress, you will notice longer dry periods or fully dry periods. This is when you know they are ready to begin removing the nappy. Before you remove the nappy, you will have all poo being caught in the potty or toilet.

Offering could look like this:
- Upon wake-up
- After breakfast
- Before and after morning nap if still napping
- After lunch (and before afternoon nap if combined)
- After afternoon nap
- After dinner (before bath/bed – often combined)
- At adult bedtime (if offering a dream pee)
- Before any vehicle journey or upon arrival if some distance.

112

Is your child getting too big for the potty? Or is your child still comfortable on the potty? Remember to graduate to the toilet (with or without a seat insert), as this will make offering the toilet during outings easier. There may be a time where you use all options you have or ask your toddler which one they would like to use. The sitting potty is still handy if your toddler likes to keep busy while sitting. The toilet makes life easier, as it is one less thing to clean.

12 months+ stages and transitions

Non-verbal dialogue

If you've been teaching some non-verbal dialogue such as baby sign language, your toddler may use some of the signs by this age. Pay extra attention to their communication for their elimination requirements. Not all toddlers will sign for the potty; don't worry if this is the case. Natural non-verbal signals around this age may include putting their hand near their crotch or jiggling, going quiet or hiding.

I am busy! Keep guiding me, but allow me some decisions!

Verbal dialogue

While communicating that it is toilet time, offer options. "It's time to go toilet. Would you like to use the potty or the toilet?" If you specifically ask them if they need to go to the toilet, they may just say no. Toddlers live in the moment and may respond with a 'no' if they are playing. Rephrase to "It's toilet time – we can come back to this activity afterwards", or an if/then statement – "*If* you potty now, *then* we can go to playgroup."

Progression toward underwear

From 12 months on, there are many developments. Your toddler is now more mobile and starting to become more independent. Because our home situations and babies are different, the steps and timeframe toward toilet independence can vary. I will try to offer options and alternatives during this section in consideration of the variables.

The next step is bladder control during the daytime. When your toddler is comfortable with the big toilet, you could pack away the potty. Generally, children with older siblings will transition to the big toilet with more confidence. By now, you will most likely be able to use toilet paper to wipe up and may only need wipes for outings. Cleaning up is getting easier!

As your little one becomes more independent, you will notice they might want to do things by themselves, such as getting onto the toilet or dressing. It can be hard to step back and let them try, but they will be eager and determined to succeed, so to avoid a power struggle, it's best to let them try on their own.

They may also begin to develop a sense of privacy around the use of the toilet, which is very natural. Ensure that the toilet set-up is accessible for them if they do happen to take themselves. Set up a more private potty area that they can access. Help them to the toilet, and then step away. Sometimes, you need to pay less attention to what they are doing, to give them space while being in the same room or nearby.

This will eventually lead to them heading to the toilet on their own. Trainer underwear will work great at this stage, and your toddler should be able to manage their removal. Spend some time showing your toddler how to remove trainers.

Placing a potty in a place visible to them can be a helpful prompt to remember to use the potty. When they are big enough, they will be interested to tip the potty contents into the toilet and flush it away. This is all important progress, as getting their involvement gives them some control and ownership.

At this point, it is still helpful to remind them to use the toilet at transitional times and after eating. You can see if they will initiate this, but don't expect too much from them and offer if they forget. This process can take some time.

Boys will also learn that they can urinate while standing up. You can teach this using a cup or similar, and it is handy if they suddenly need to urinate when they get into bath water. Warm water and running water will often trigger urination. Clip-on urinals are an excellent option for boys when they are not tall enough to reach the toilet bowl or encourage them to stand on the step-stool. Things can get a little messy when they are learning. Remember to teach them to point down and aim.

Transition into underwear

The first part of toilet learning should be understood for all children before removing the nappy/trainer back-up. They should understand where to go toilet and be showing signs of dryness.

At this time, remove the absorbent back-up (during the day) and commit – don't look back. Communicate this with your child! You can still wear back-up during naps and overnight unless you are tackling this all at once.

There is *no* set end age.
Be patient, each child
will reach this milestone
when they do.

Choose a period where you can be at home or easily manage a flood and a change of clothes. Our little ones are often rushed through the busy week with daycare or playgroups, and outings. Take a 'home holiday' to concentrate on the transition to underwear. Slow down your pace for a while. It will probably be good for you too. Keep things simple over this period, such as a visit to your local playground. This is also a good strategy if you have some regression. At home, your little one can reset their focus and have your full attention to help with the toilet. It can help them get back on track or progress them along.

Make it a special experience when your child gets their first underwear. Let your child learn by natural consequence, by becoming wet. They will experience wetting themselves without a safety net a few times before it registers. Oversee them carefully over this time and remind them when it's time to go to the toilet. Toddlers will often put their hands near their crotch if they need to go. Have a potty visible for your child, such as one set up near their play area if the toilet is not handy.

Is your toddler still showing periods of dryness while wearing underwear, or is your child flooding them often? If the flooding is frequent, you may need to take a step back to absorbent back-up. It is not a flood if it's just a little bit of wetting (some children, more commonly boys, dribble a little). This issue tends to right itself over time.

The thought of your toddler flooding in your house may make you cringe, especially if your home has carpet.

If weather permits, spend time in your garden or at a nearby playground. You may want to place rugs or a foam mat around their play area over this time. If you have to clean up pee from the carpet, here is an easy method.

It's all about ME now – PEE! Weeeeeeeeeee! Help them remember not to spill me!

To remove pee from carpet
Dilute: Wet down the area with warm water to dilute the pee and use a towel, pressing firmly to absorb.
Clean: Mix white vinegar with some warm water and salt to remove the odour.
Rinse: Repeat the first step and use dry towels to absorb as much of the water as possible.

Don't forget to pack a change of pants and underwear now in your car and bag. The process can take some time. You will need to balance your assistance with their lead. This is an important stage where you will be stepping back more and more over time as they take over their toilet management. You'll still need to wipe up though – you're not off the hook just yet. It's important to remember to be their back-up and remind them when they do get busy.

Line your car seat and pram or pushchair with a waterproof pad to save a big clean-up job.

During this stage, make sure your toddler is dressed in clothing that is easy to remove. Jeans – no, trackpants –

yes. Don't make it difficult for your little one to access the toilet by putting them in clothing that is difficult to handle.

Watch out for excessive holding on

Excessive holding on (to poo) can sometimes develop into constipation, which can lead to other issues if the situation is chronic. A severe blockage of very firm stool can cause wetting accidents and bedwetting.

Constipation can happen to anyone, and observation, healthy toilet practice and a healthy diet are ways to avoid this issue. If a toddler has experienced a hard stool after medication or if it is diet-related, the connection that poo is painful could cause them to withhold further, making the situation worse. Toilet anxiety is another contributor. Anxiety over a particular toilet, such as a toilet at daycare or fear of noisy public toilets where hand dryers or other people in the room could be startling, could cause toilet anxiety. Stress when transitioning from using a nappy to using a toilet could be challenging, especially when the child is training at a more self-aware stage. Further anxiety can arise when a child is self-aware with chronic constipation and wetting themselves. It is essential to treat their constipation and also their anxiety.

Be watchful where you notice your child hiding to poo. The behaviour of hiding while defecating before completion of toilet training is associated with stool toileting refusal, constipation, and stool withholding. These behaviours may make toilet training more difficult.[38] A later age at initiation of toilet training, stool toileting refusal, and constipation may explain some of the trend toward completion of toilet training at later ages.[39]

If you are worried that your child has not passed stool for some time, first try giving them foods that will help get things moving. High-fibre foods, including fruits and fruit juices that contain sorbitol (prune, mango, pear), vegetables (broccoli, peas), beans, and whole-grain bread and cereals, are important in their diet. Kiwifruit are effective, as is prune juice (a mild, natural laxative that works for some children). A quick rule of thumb – fruit that starts with 'p' can help move poo. Only offer them foods which they have had before if you are concerned with potential food allergies. Seek medical advice if the problem persists, as prolonging constipation can cause further issues.

Elimination Communication encourages observation and regular toilet assistance. Keep a mental note on how often your child is passing stool; one a day is regular and healthy for many children around this age. Some children (and adults too!) only feel comfortable doing a poo at home, so allow time in your day at home. Ensuring that your child is comfortable in new toilet environments, such as at a daycare or preschool, is important. Take them to the toilet everywhere, and stay with them while they use the toilet. This is very important when they are starting in care. Spend time with them using the toilet in the new centre if you can, so it feels comfortable for them.

If they experience a set-back with Elimination Communication when starting in care, work through this with the child and discuss their anxieties. Introduce a toddler book about the potty, and discuss that it is a normal bodily function and important. Give them time, offer privacy if they need it, or sit with them if they need you. Read some books or sing some songs. Keep toilet time stress free. Keeping them regular with stool is important and healthy. Keeping your own toilet anxieties under control is important for your child as well. You may not like the dirtiness of public toilets (very understandable), but keep any negative opinions quiet so that they don't concern your impressionable child.

When you are travelling but nearly home and your child asks to go to the toilet, it's OK to ask them to hold on (within reason) as you know the child will understand their relief will come soon. But don't encourage holding on when it's not an emergency. Always remember to offer the opportunity to go to the toilet regularly. With observation, practice in many toilet locations, a good diet and regular toilet breaks, your child will most likely avoid issues.

Starting EC from 12 months+

We're going to take a slightly different approach when starting Elimination Communication from 12 months as we are entering the final stage toward toilet independence which is essentially the toilet training stage.

To start, we will want to become familiar with the toilet (or potty). Start by introducing the concept, demonstrate yourself or use a sibling or role-play. Then start by offering the toilet routinely after eating as mentioned in previous stages. If nothing happens in the potty, and you are able to do so, keep the nappy off and start to observe your toddler. Set up play in an area close to the potty for easy access. As soon as they show any indication they are about to eliminate, bring them to the toilet or potty. Offer your full attention. Bring out the toys that they have not seen for a while. You can use a cue for pee and poo or just your words at this age. They will appreciate positive encouragement. It's now important to keep this consistent for them.

Keep calm about any misses. Communication is important. Explain why we now use the toilet.

Removing the nappy removes their 'toilet', so they will either wait until a nappy or trainers are put back on to eliminate or learn to use a potty. We're aiming for them to use the potty or toilet. If you can focus on doing this after each snack and meal for a week, you will make significant progress. Put the underwear back on after they have gone toilet.

Understanding when your child usually poos can be beneficial. Remove the back-up around their typical poo time, and as soon as you see any signals, guide them to the toilet or potty and hope for the best! Remember, it may feel strange for them to use the potty for a poo when they have been used to using the nappy all their life.

They may not associate the toilet with elimination for some time as they go through this period of relearning. All children have natural signals which indicate they need to eliminate such as wriggling, staring or glassy eyes, refusing food, breaking wind, putting their hands down near their nappy or tugging on the nappy. Make the most of their natural signals, and offer the toilet at these times.

This stage for you is all about toilet elimination association. Don't rush this stage, go gentle and easy and offer consistently. This will require your dedication and assistance. Once you have established use of the toilet or potty, continue offering guidance until you're also starting to see more prolonged periods of dryness. Then move into the toilet independence stage and removing their (daytime) back-up completely.

Naps and nighttime 12 months+

Liquids

If your little one is still comfort feeding, consider that it will result in more toilet requirements or a possible nappy change. Generally, you will want to reduce liquid intake about an hour before naps or two hours before bedtime if possible. If your child loves a drink bottle beside the bed, offer a small amount. If your child is still nursing at night, generally offer before nursing during the night, then nurse back to sleep – however, do what works for you.

Wind down

Create a bedtime routine that involves you helping your little one get ready for bed, including bathroom duties, followed by quiet reading time. Make sure they go to the bathroom before bedtime.

Dream pee

If you offer opportunities during the night, keep the offer quick (no longer than a minute so that they stay drowsy), keep the room dimly lit and warm and cue them on to pee. Two-piece pyjamas will be easier for offering at nighttime. You could start with a couple of timed offers, e.g. 10 pm (this could be your bedtime), then again at 2 am and adjust as you need to.

- Offer at their bedtime.
- Offer at your bedtime.
- Offer at feeding times, if still night feeding.
- Offer first thing in the morning.

Encourage independence

Once your toddler is in a toddler bed, teach them to go to the bathroom at nighttime when they need to go. Encourage them and offer your assistance if they need it. Put night lights from the bedroom to the bathroom or a potty in the bedroom. Place a vinyl play mat beneath the potty in case of spills.

A little progress each day adds up to big results.

Preparation

To avoid a full bed change during the night, make the bed in sheet/liner layers and remove only the wet affected sheet and liner if an accident occurs. Keep spare PJs (night wear) handy near the bed for a quick night change.

Remove back-up

Once your toddler is waking up dry most mornings, trial underwear or thicker trainer underwear. It's hard to say what age this will happen for you, based on how much nighttime assistance you have given. It's important that wetting during the night does not become a habit. Removing that nighttime nappy is an exciting step in growing up. Be mindful when your little one is sick or in a new bedroom, such as an unfamiliar room (accommodation). These are times when you might experience a nighttime bedwetting accident, so consider a back-up at times like these.

Sleep

When your child changes their sleep pattern (drops a day sleep, for example), they will go through a period of adjustment and are likely to be quite tired at certain times of the day. This can lead to accidents, so be wary of when your child is struggling with awareness.

Never let a stumble in the road be the end of the journey.

Setbacks

Setbacks can happen at any stage, but the 10–13 month stage is the most common time for pushback, power struggles or setbacks. Here are a few reasons setbacks can happen and what you can do to help get things back on track.

Being busy

Being busy, watching TV, playing – all can lead to a child having an accident. Some children will hold off going to the toilet and then 'leak' a little of their full bladder. Reminding busy children and taking busy children to the bathroom at regular intervals, such as after snack and meal times, will help. If your child says they don't need to go – they quite often just want to keep playing – remind them they can keep playing after they eat and go to the bathroom.

A medical issue

Any medical issue with the genitals may lead to accidents or urine not going in the right direction, which could cause some anxiety around toilet practice. Illness, or other medical issues, may also affect toilet practice. If necessary, seek medical advice. Health comes first. It's OK to pause toilet learning and pick it up again when things have settled.

Power struggles

As your toddler reaches an independent stage, they may test their boundaries, which is an important step as they learn to become their own person. You may be hit with a complete rejection of going to the toilet. Keep offering the opportunity, but never force them. You can try a little motivation, such as, "After you go to the toilet and wash up, then we can…". Negotiating with toddlers can be tricky. You're also trying to encourage their independence, so it is a balancing act.

Taking turns might help. "My turn first" – they might want to go first and decide it's their turn. Sometimes pushing a toddler will only be met with just as much pushing back, and the battle is not worth it. Sometimes a small break is all they need before trying again.

Try giving your child some control over the situation, like allowing them to take their underwear off or allowing them to flush. This will provide them with a sense of being 'big' and doing it themselves. Remind them how 'big' they are getting and how impressed you are that they can do things by themselves. They will love to hear how pleased you are with their efforts. As with all power struggles, allowing your little one some control or power will most likely alleviate their frustrations.

Don't ask if they need to go to the toilet, instead say, "It's time to go to the potty." Asking them a question can give you an automatic refusal, even when it is clear they need to go. Start to offer options so that they can participate in decisions. Would you like to use this potty or the toilet with a seat insert? Use directive language to guide them, as it helps at this age.

Redirecting

If your toddler is using a specific location to poo, you can place a potty in that location as a prompt but they will most likely need assistance. If the location is another sitting place, be vigilant and watch for their natural signals, then ask them to wait until you can take them to the potty. Explain why we use a toilet.

If your toddler is arching their back or straightening their legs, see if you can remove the trainers and leave a potty nearby. Step back, lay out toys and observe. Encourage role-play or try reading a book to them, as this can encourage them to sit longer on a potty or toilet.

Keeping your calm

If the struggle is overwhelming, take a breath. Check in on yourself. Are you pushing too much? Are you stressed? Pull things back to the basics of just offering after meals, or take a short break. Prompt, or set them up to potty and then step back and let them process it.

Dealing with change 12 months+

If there has been a big change in your child's life, this could cause a setback. You can choose a quiet time to sit down with your child to discuss the change and ask if they are concerned or upset about it. Helping them through their anxiety will help get them back on track with toilet practice. Use lots of praise for success.

One of the most common changes will be a new family member. By pottying the newborn and the toddler together, it can become a shared experience. Don't neglect your toddler's toilet needs. It can be harder to juggle with a newborn, but you will manage this incredibly special and busy time. Get them involved in the process to help their sibling.

Introducing a caregiver to EC

If your toddler is starting care from 12 months and has established the use of the potty or toilet, introducing this routine to a caregiver should be straightforward. Introduce the new toilet environment to your toddler yourself to help them settle in. It can be helpful if you offer the toilet when you arrive or just before you leave for some time to help them adjust. Your daycare provider can then start to offer the toilet after meals and after naps. They may have a nappy change routine. Take a look and see if this would be similar to your potty routine. Maintain the toilet practice, but don't worry about wet nappies until they are ready for the next steps.

When you are sharing care duties, it is best to be as consistent as possible. The free *Elimination Communication Log* app can be a helpful tool to track their progress and elimination.

Once they've transitioned to using the toilet, going to the toilet when out and about becomes easier. With toddlers, it pays to know where a toilet is at any given time. If they need to use the toilet, they often need to use it immediately.

Pack a change of clothing in case of accidents, and a wet bag. Line the car seat and the pushchair with a waterproof pad just in case.

Hiking

Clip a potty to the pack and bring wet bags, toilet paper, and a small spade if facilities are inconvenient. Cloth nappies can be washed and dried quickly if it is an overnight excursion. Offer frequently when you are having breaks and snacks or meals. Your pack and waste load will be lighter than bringing along disposables or having to deal with soiled cloth.

Photo @BackToTheWildNZ

Public toilets

Public toilets make most of us cringe, but try not to share that feeling with your toddler. Using public toilets will be a good experience for them as long as you're calm and matter of fact about the experience.

Long-distance

It can be best to revert back to wearing an absorbent pull-up or trainers for long-distance travel. Try to offer the toilet as you would at home when you can or need a toilet break yourself. Toilet before leaving and upon arrival.

Vehicles

By now, your toddler may prefer privacy – if this is the case, try to use public facilities instead of a potty in the vehicle, unless of course there are no other options.

Nature calls

Let's face it, at some point, we're going to pee in nature. Find a private spot, and don't leave any evidence behind. Travel potty with bags or dog poo bags are convenient for any waste or wipes.

Milestones 12 months+

- Using the big toilet, learning to get on and off and how to flush.

- Learning to wash hands independently after toilet use.

- Graduating from nappies to underwear.

- Telling you they need to go toilet.

Tips 12 months+

- Get a good waterproof mattress cover.

- Reward your little one with 'big kid' underwear they will be impressed with. They deserve a great reward for their efforts!

- Take spare clothes on outings as your child transitions into underwear.

- Go buy yourself a nice treat too – you are saving yourself loads of money, helping the environment and helping your child be more self-aware.

PFFTT...
I can see when
I'm not wanted!
Well, not with you
lot... but there
are plenty of
others who still
love me!

Well done! We share EC stories and would love to hear about your experience! Sharing inspires others.
Find us online @eliminationcommunicationbabies.
We hope this book has helped you along your EC journey!

My first
#liquidgold
on a potty!

AWARDED TO / AGE

VERIFIED BY

DATE

Elimination
Communication
Babies

My first
#solidgold
on a potty!

AWARDED TO / AGE

VERIFIED BY

Elimination
Communication
Babies

DATE

I'm a
nappy grad!
#undies4me

AWARDED TO / AGE

VERIFIED BY

DATE

Elimination
Communication
Babies

Spread the good

Through the combined efforts of all Elimination Communication Babies, EC and cloth communities, we are significantly reducing landfill waste in countries around the world.

Both you and your little one have learned a lot through the process, and your commitment will have given your little one dignity and confidence in their toilet-practice ability.

We wish you all the best as you continue your parenting journey through this stage and onto the next.

Errors and omissions – Apologies if you find any errors or omissions. I aim to write this to help parents as best I can. If you do find a mistake or something left out, I would be grateful for your feedback to eliminationcommunciationbabies@gmail.com
Your reviews also really help lift our spirits, and share our efforts.

Thank you for taking the EC journey with us!
We love seeing your wins! If you're inspired to get involved further with our efforts to share EC, we would love to hear from you and invite working collaboratively with like-minded parents.

We invite you to join our Facebook group.
Elimination Communication Babies Support.
Connect with other parents who are choosing
elimination communication for their baby.

Find us at
Facebook @EliminationCommunicationBabies
Instagram #EliminationCommunicationBabies
YouTube Elimination Communication Babies
Redbubble ECBabies

Celebrate your #solidgoldwin and
#liquidgoldwin with us as you go!
It's fun!

EC is cool
'cause babies can potty!

References

1   HOLSENBACK H., SMITH L., STEVENSON MD. Cutaneous abscesses in children: epidemiology in the era of methicillin-resistant Staphylococcus aureus in a pediatric emergency department. *Pediatr Emerg Care.* 2012;28(7):684–686

2   DUONG TH., JANSSON UB., HOLMDAHL G., SILLÉN U., HELLSTROM AL. Development of bladder control in the first year of life in children who are potty trained early. *J Pediatr Urol.* 2010;6(5):501–505pmid:19939737

3   DUONG TH., JANSSON UB., HOLMDAHL G., SILLÉN U., HELLSTROM AL. Development of bladder control in the first year of life in children who are potty trained early. *J Pediatr Urol.* 2010;6(5):501–505pmid:19939737

4   DUONG TH., JANSSON UB., HOLMDAHL G., SILLÉN U., HELLSTROM AL. Development of bladder control in the first year of life in children who are potty trained early. *J Pediatr Urol.* 2010;6(5):501–505pmid:19939737

5   DEWAR G. (2010) The science of toilet training: what research tells us about timing. www.parentingscience.com

6   ESTRADA-ZAMBRANO N. (2020) Elimination Communication Research Study and Survey

7   RUGOLOTTO S., SUN M., BOUCKE L., CALÒ DG., TATÒ L. Toilet training started during the first year of life: a report on elimination signals, stool toileting refusal and completion age. *Minerva Pediatr.* 2008 Feb;60(1):27-35. PMID: 18277362.

8   BENDER J., SHE R. (2017) Elimination Communication: Diaper free in America. *Pediatrics. Official Journal of the American Academy of Pediatrics.* www.pediatricsaappublications.org

9   ESTRADA-ZAMBRANO N. (2020) Elimination Communication Research Study and Survey

10 BRAZELTON TB. A child-oriented approach to toilet training. *Pediatrics.* 1962;29:121–128pmid:13872676

11 Real Diaper Association (2021) Diaper Facts and Statistics in 2021. www.realdiapers.org/diaper-facts

12 BARKSDALE N. (2020) Who Invented the Flush Toilet? www.history.com

13 STAMP J. (2014) From Turrets to Toilets: A Partial History of the Throne Room. www.smithsonianmag.com

14 DEWAR G. (2010) The science of toilet training: what research tells us about timing. www.parentingscience.com

15 ENGELHART K. (2014) The Powerful History of Potty Training. www.theatlantic.com

16 ENGELHART K. (2014) The Powerful History of Potty Training. www.theatlantic.com

17 ENGELHART K. (2014) The Powerful History of Potty Training. www.theatlantic.com

18 BENTLEY A. (2014) *Inventing Baby Food*. University of California Press, p59.

19 MORIN GV. Inventor; Chicopee Manufacturing Corporation, assignee. Waterproof disposable diaper. United States Patent US 2699170 A. January 11,1955

20 BRAZELTON TB. A child-oriented approach to toilet training. *Pediatrics*. 1962;29:121–128pmid:13872676

21 ENGELHART K. (2014) The Powerful History of Potty Training. www.theatlantic.com

22 BENDER J., SHE R. (2017) Elimination Communication: Diaper free in America. *Pediatrics. Official Journal of the American Academy of Pediatrics*. www.pediatricsaappublications.org

23 ENGELHART K. (2014) The Powerful History of Potty Training. www.theatlantic.com

24 DUONG TH., JANSSON UB., HOLMDAHL G., SILLÉN U., HELLSTROM AL. Development of bladder control in the first year of life in children who are potty trained early. *J Pediatr Urol*. 2010;6(5):501–505pmid:19939737

25 BEAUDRY-BELLEFEUILLE I., BOOTH D., LANE SJ. Defecation-Specific Behavior in Children with Functional Defecation Issues: A Systematic Review. *Perm J*. 2017;21:17-047. doi: 10.7812/TPP/17-047. PMID: 29035187; PMCID: PMC5638627.

26 ESTRADA-ZAMBRANO N. (2020) Elimination Communication Research Study and Survey

27 ESTRADA-ZAMBRANO N. (2020) Elimination Communication Research Study and Survey

28 DUONG TH., JANSSON UB., HOLMDAHL G., SILLÉN U., HELLSTRÖM AL. Urinary bladder control during the first 3 years of life in healthy children in Vietnam--a comparison study with Swedish children. *J Pediatr Urol*. 2013 Dec;9(6 Pt A):700-6. doi: 10.1016/j.jpurol.2013.04.022. Epub 2013 Jun 10. PMID: 23759503.

29 ESTRADA-ZAMBRANO N. (2020) Elimination Communication Research Study and Survey

30 DUONG TH., JANSSON UB., HOLMDAHL G., SILLÉN U., HELLSTROM AL. Development of bladder control in the first year of life in children who are potty trained early. *J Pediatr Urol*. 2010;6(5):501–505pmid:19939737

31 RUGOLOTTO S., SUN M., BOUCKE L., CALÒ DG., TATÒ L. Toilet training started during the first year of life: a report on elimination signals, stool toileting refusal and completion age. *Minerva Pediatr*. 2008 Feb;60(1):27-35. PMID: 18277362.

32 ESTRADA-ZAMBRANO N. (2020) Elimination Communication Research Study and Survey

33 ESTRADA-ZAMBRANO N. (2020) Elimination Communication Research Study and Survey

34 Real Diaper Association (2021) Diaper Facts and Statistics in 2021. www.realdiapers.org/diaper-facts

35 ESTRADA-ZAMBRANO N. (2020) Elimination Communication Research Study and Survey

36 JORDAN GJ. Elimination communication as colic therapy. *Med Hypotheses*. 2014 Sep;83(3):282-5. doi: 10.1016/j.mehy.2014.05.018. Epub 2014 Jun 7. PMID: 24962210.

37 BENDER J., SHE R. (2017) Elimination Communication: Diaper free in America. *Pediatrics. Official Journal of the American Academy of Pediatrics.* www.pediatricsaappublications.org

38 TAUBMAN B., BLUM NJ., NEMETH N. Children who hide while defecating before they have completed toilet training: a prospective study. *Arch Pediatr Adolesc Med.* 2003 Dec;157(12):1190-2. doi: 10.1001/archpedi.157.12.1190. PMID: 14662572.

39 BLUM NJ., TAUBMAN B., NEMETH N. Why is toilet training occurring at older ages? A study of factors associated with later training. *J Pediatr*. 2004 Jul;145(1):107-11. doi: 10.1016/j.jpeds.2004.02.022. PMID: 15238916.

Additional resources and further reading

Elimination Communication
Visit our blog for stories, research and product reviews for Elimination Communication.
EliminationCommunicationBabies.com

Baby language
Education – How to recognise and understand a newborn's communication.
DunstanBabyLanguage.com

Breastfeeding
La Leche League International – International organisation with local chapters you can join for information and support with breastfeeding.
llli.org

Environmental
Waste-free living and cloth nappy solutions (New Zealand).
katemeads.co.nz

First 1000 days
App to support activities and learning through the first 1000 days.
oliikiapp.com

US organisation to promote the benefits for a baby's first 1000 days.
thousanddays.org

Toilet learning
Coaching, seminars and products for toilet learning (New Zealand).
looloo.co.nz

Invitation to collaborate
If your business or organisation's philosophy falls in line with ours, please contact
eliminationcommunicationbabies@gmail.com to see how we can support one another.